Contents

Colour Basics for GIS Users

Allan Brown and Wim Feringa

An imprint of Pearson Education

Harlow, England • London • New York • Boston • San Francisco • Toronto
Sydney • Tokyo • Singapore • Hong Kong • Seoul • Taipei • New Delhi
Cape Town • Madrid • Mexico City • Amsterdam • Munich • Paris • Milan

Pearson Education Limited
Edinburgh Gate
Harlow
Essex CM20 2JE
England

and Associated Companies throughout the world

Visit us on the World Wide Web at:
www.pearsoneduc.com

First published 2003

Learning Resources
Centre

ISBN 0 130 33343 3

British Library Cataloguing-in-Publication Data
A catalogue record for this book is available from the British Library

Library of Congress Cataloging-in-Publication Data
Brown, Allan, 1943-
    Colour basics for GIS users / Allan Brown and Wim Feringa.
        p. cm.
    Includes bibliographical references (p.).
    ISBN 0-13-033343-3 (pbk.)
    1. Geographic information systems. 2. Color computer graphics. I. Title: Colour
basics for Geographic Information System users. II. Feringa, Wim. III. Title.

G70.212 .B76 2002
025.06'91—dc21   2002072927

10   9   8   7   6   5   4   3   2   1
06   05   04   03   02

Cover, text design and illustrations by Wim Feringa

Typeset by 35 in 9.7/12.5pt BakerSignetBT
Printed in China
EPC/01

Preface

As a Geographic Information System user, you have no doubt
often been faced with the task of visualising the results of a
complex analysis. You know that careful use of colour can help,
but you are perhaps not sure how best to choose the colours.
Then, after much effort has produced an acceptable image on the
computer display screen, you are very disappointed when the
printed result looks quite different. This book has been compiled
with these situations in mind.

In recent years, coloured graphics have become increasingly
popular due to the ready availability of GIS and graphic software
for use on a PC even by the relatively inexperienced user. Graphic
boards offering millions of colours and colour output devices such
as high resolution colour graphic screens and printers can be
purchased at low prices. However, the easy accessibility to the
application of colour also has its drawbacks. People who may
have little experience have (almost) unlimited freedom to select
and use colour. The temptation is often to overuse colour to get
a kaleidoscopic result, yet without improving the communicative
qualities of the map. Furthermore the colours may appear quite
different when printed on paper. It is therefore necessary that the
GIS user and mapmaker should have at least a basic knowledge of
colour vision, colour technology and the application of colour on
maps.

This book begins with an introductory chapter on the challenges
involved in the use of colour in GIS and cartography. This is
followed by an explanation of how colour is created and how the
human eye-brain combination perceives colour. The colours that
we see can be modelled as three-dimensional spaces. Some of
the more important of these spaces, those that are relevant to
the practical user of colour, are then described briefly. Input of
colour data into a digital system, colour manipulation and output
on display screens and on paper, together with the problems of
transferring colour accurately from one to the other, are dealt with
in some detail. Colour charts can be useful in this regard. Their
design and use are described, using as an example the ITC colour
chart. The book concludes with hints and examples on the use of
colour on GIS visualisations and maps.

In addition to original material, much has been compiled from various existing sources. The authors hope that bringing diverse information together in one book will provide a useful basic reference for GIS users and cartographers. Readers are however warned that some of the technical information may become outdated quickly, and they should refer to journals, trade magazines and the Internet for the latest developments. A companion website to the book (http://kartoweb.itc.nl/colour) contains updated technical information and links to other sources, with some emphasis on those sites offering interactive colour programs and demonstrations. Alternative URLs will be given in case any of the URLs listed at the end of the book become unavailable. In addition, the site contains those book illustrations where it is useful to be able to compare the colours of the display screen version with those of the printed version.

Acknowledgements

This book has grown out of the materials used in teaching colour in the cartography and GIS courses at the International Institute for Aerospace Survey and Earth Sciences (ITC) in Enschede, the Netherlands (in January 2002 the ITC changed its full name to the International Institute for Geo-information Science and Earth Observation). Our thanks are due to the Institute and in particular to Prof. Menno-Jan Kraak, as head of the Division of Geoinformatics, Cartography and Visualisation, for allowing us time to work on the book. Several colleagues and students of the Division assisted us by reading the text at various stages and by making critical comments. We are especially grateful in this regard to Corné van Elzakker, Richard Knippers, Etien Koua, Anu Shrestha and Jeroen van den Worm.

Two academic colleagues in the United Kingdom, David Forrest of Glasgow University and David Green of Aberdeen University, used an early version of the book, published internally, in their teaching. They made useful comments and suggestions for improvement and they also encouraged us to approach an academic publisher. Matthew Smith of Pearson Education responded favourably and assisted us in many ways in the longer than expected process of improving and extending the early version of the text. No doubt being used to dealing with technical authors he did not press us too hard even after one deadline after another passed!

Allan Brown and Wim Feringa

Enschede
November, 2001

Abbreviations and acronyms

ASCII	American Standard Code for Information Interchange
bit	binary digit
CAD	Computer-Aided Design
CCD	Charge Coupled Device
CIE	Commission Internationale d'Eclairage
CIS	Contact Image Sensor
CMYK	Cyan, Magenta, Yellow, Black
CRT	Cathode Ray Tube
DEM	Digital Elevation Model
DIN	Deutsches Institut für Normung
DMD	Digital Micromirror Device
dpi	dots per inch
DTP	Desk Top Publishing
DXF	Data Exchange File
EL	Electroluminescent Panel
EPS	Encapsulated PostScript
FED	Field Emission Display
FPD	Flat Panel Display
FST	Flat Square Tube
GCR	Grey Component Replacement
GIF	Graphics Interchange Format
GIS	Geographical Information System
GPS	Global Positioning System
GPU	Graphics Processing Unit
HCI	Hue, Chroma, Intensity
hex	hexadecimal
HIS	Intensity, Hue, Saturation
HLS	Hue, Luminance, Saturation
HPGL	Hewlett-Packard Graphics Language
HSB	Hue, Saturation, Brightness
HSV	Hue, Saturation, Value
HTML	Hypertext Markup Language
Hz	Hertz
ICC	International Colour Consortium
ISCC	Inter-Society Color Council
ITC	International Institute for Aerospace Survey and Earth Sciences (from January 2002 the International Institute for Geo-information Science and Earth Observation)

JPEG	Joint Photographic Experts Group
LCD	Liquid Crystal Display
LED	Light-Emitting Diode
lpi	lines per inch
LUT	Lookup Table
MSS	Multi-Spectral Scanner
NBS	(American) National Bureau of Standards
NCS	Natural Colour System
PDF	Portable Document Format
PDL	Page Description Language
PDP	Plasma Display Panel
pixel	picture element
PNG	Portable Network Graphics
PS	PostScript
RAMDAC	Random Access Memory Digital-to-Analogue Converter
RGB	Red, Green, Blue
RIP	Raster Image Processor
SVG	Scalable Vector Graphics
TFT	Thin Film Transistor
TIFF	Tagged Image File Format
UCR	Under Colour Removal
URL	Universal Resource Locator
VFD	Vacuum Fluorescent Display
WMF	Windows Metafile Format
WYSIWYG	What You See Is What You Get
XML	Extensible Markup Language

Trademark notice

The following are trademarks or registered trademarks of their respective companies:

Acrobat, Acrobat Reader, Illustrator, PageMaker, Photoshop and PostScript are trademarks of Adobe Systems Inc; Apple and Macintosh are trademarks of Apple Computer, Inc; Arc/Info, Atlas GIS and ArcView are trademarks of ESRI; Bentley and MicroStation are trademarks of Bentley Systems, Inc; CorelDRAW is a trademark of Corel Corporation; LaserJet and DeskJet are trademarks of Hewlett Packard Corporation; ElectroInk is a trademark of Indigo N.V; ERDAS IMAGINE is a trademark of ERDAS, Inc; Focoltone Colour System is a trademark of Focoltone; FreeHand and Shockwave are trademarks of Macromedia, Inc; ILWIS is a trademark of the ITC (distributed commercially by PCI, Canada); Microsoft and Windows are trademarks of Microsoft Corporation; Pantone is a trademark of Pantone Inc; QuarkXPress is a trademark of Quark, Inc; Trinitron is a trademark of Sony Electronics, Inc; Color Finder is a trademark of the Toyo Ink Mfg. Co; Trumatch is a trademark of Trumatch, Inc.

Publisher's acknowledgements

We are grateful to the following for permission to reproduce copyright material:

Scandinavian Colour Institute AB for Figures 3.8 and 3.9. Scandinavian Colour Institute AB hold all legal rights to NCS and NCS System™®; Muster-Schmidt GmbH for Figure 3.12; Dr Patrick Herzog for Figure 3.22.

While every effort has been made to trace the owners of copyright material, in a few cases this has proved impossible and we would be grateful to hear from anyone with information which would enable us to do so.

Chapter 1

The use of colour in GIS and cartography – the challenge

Colour in GIS and graphics software

The results of an analysis within a Geographic Information System (GIS) are very often presented as a map or other graphic on a computer monitor or printed on paper. Furthermore, most cartographers these days compile and design their maps on screen. This is now the standard method for producing printed maps and in some cases, e.g. on the Internet, the screen is the final medium for presentation. To make these maps and graphics, GIS users and cartographers will normally use one or more commercial software packages. These packages will often allow very free use of colour but usually without any guide for the user as to how best to use this facility.

There tends to be a fundamental difference in approach between GIS software packages such as Arc/Info and graphics packages such as Adobe Illustrator, CorelDRAW or Macromedia FreeHand. The GIS packages are primarily concerned with the manipulation of spatial data, often leading to the preparation of a map or graphic on the screen. They normally include a very simple conversion to create output colours on paper, usually produced by an inkjet or laser printer. The fact that the colours on the printed version may appear very different from the screen colours does not seem to be of much concern. The graphics packages, on the other hand, are very much concerned with the final paper version, commonly produced by offset printing or direct printing from digital files to special printing systems. In these packages, therefore, an attempt is made to match the colours on the screen to the final printed colours. In order to attain an even better match, the larger commercial graphics arts companies employ expensive and complex colour management systems.

GIS users and cartographers vary a good deal in their requirements concerning colour. Some are quite happy with just a few very distinctive colours and do not care much if these turn out to be rather different when printed, possibly because only they will use the result. At the other extreme are those who are designing complex graphic images with careful, systematic application of colour for other people to use. This category may find it very difficult to produce an acceptable result on paper just by using the standard GIS software. They may therefore decide to do the final design using graphics software, with all the attendant problems of transferring files from one software package to another. The aim of this book is to assist in the use of colour these two extreme user types and all those in between.

How to use colour?

At one time, producing a coloured graphic was a much more expensive and time-consuming operation than producing a monochrome (i.e. black and white) one. Furthermore, there was often no alternative to monochrome – until recently, for example, full coloured illustrations were not possible in newspapers. This meant that even if the production system allowed it there had to be a real need or at least a significant advantage in using colour in order to justify the extra expense. Nowadays, the PCs used for GIS and cartography are equipped with colour monitors as standard. Coloured paper output produced by inkjet or laser printers is relatively cheap, at least for small numbers of copies in small formats. Even the formerly rather expensive offset printing process, especially suitable for multicolour printing, long runs and large formats, is becoming steadily cheaper due to technical developments. In other words, the economic barriers to using colour are coming down. But does this mean that just because we are less restricted in the use of colours we can use colour at will?

The French cartographer Bertin (1967) organised the perceived differences among cartographic symbols into a system of so-called visual variables. There are six of these, in addition to the position of the symbol. Five of the six non-positional variables, namely size, value, texture, orientation and form, can be applied to monochrome symbols. The remaining visual variable is colour, or, more accurately, hue. Bertin did not actually pay a great deal of attention to colour, merely noting that it should be applied to indicate nominal (categoric) differences among the features to be symbolised. This is in fact commonly the case, for example in topographic and geological maps. The coloured tint scales seen for example in rainfall or population density maps are in fact examples of the use of lightness (value) differences in order to indicate class differences, from low to high.

A topographic map is a good example of a map type that makes use of colour to differentiate among the categories of features mapped. For most of the nineteenth century the production technique was based on copper engraving, so only one colour (black) was possible for all point and line symbols and for text. Colour could be added later, but only by watercolour 'washes' manually applied to areas. The advent of light-sensitive emulsions and lithographic printing, that later developed into rotary offset printing as still used today, enabled different colours to be used for all symbols and text. This was soon seen to be a big advantage, since it made the maps much more legible. Quite quickly a more or less standardised set of colours came to be used on topographic maps produced all over the world (Figure 1.1). The basic topographic details, especially the man-made features, were usually printed in black, though red was also used in some countries. A tint of black (i.e. very small dots of black to give the impression of grey) or a separate grey ink was often used as an infill for larger buildings. Red, together with orange and yellow, were applied as road fills to indicate differences in road class. Blue became the standard for water features, a dark blue for lines and text, a light blue for open water. Contour lines and their annotation were normally printed in brown. A medium or fairly dark green came to be adopted for woodland, with perhaps a light green for permanent grassland. These colours became conventions, so familiar to users that they hardly needed to consult the map legend.

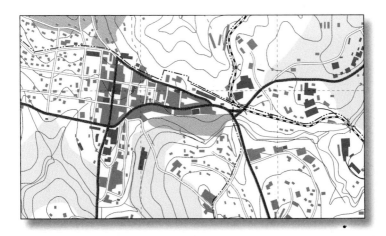

Figure 1.1 An extract from a typical topographic map

Colour conventions are also developed in other map types. Some of them were established by the scientific disciplines that produced the maps, a good example being the colours used on geological maps. Others arose by a process of imitation, for example the relief layer colour scheme still often found today, beginning with a dark green for the lowest ground and progressing up through lighter greens, beige, light brown and darker browns to purple. Although some of these conventions are not strict, still it causes confusion if the cartographer departs too far from them. As a general rule, the more the map designer can take account of user expectations regarding colour the better.

For example, it is difficult without a legend to decide what exactly is being mapped in the left hand map in Figure 1.2, apart from the clues offered by the shapes. On the right hand map the colours are familiar, at least to geographers, so the user can make a reasonable guess that it is a land use map of an urban area that includes a commercial centre, open water and parks. Population density maps often use a conventional colour value scale that begins at light yellow and progresses through oranges and reds to dark red. Rainfall maps may have a set of colours beginning with light yellow (indicating dryness) and ending with dark blue (indicating extreme wetness). Temperature maps may show a double scale, for example light yellow to dark red for increasing positive temperatures (above 0°C) and light greenish blue to dark blue for increasing negative ones (Figure 1.3). These temperature colours are based on the artistic

Figure 1.2 Random and conventional colours in land use mapping

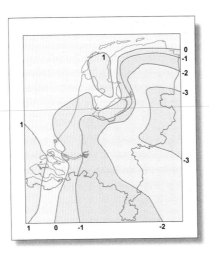

Figure 1.3 An extract from a conventionally coloured winter temperature map of Europe

idea of 'warm' reddish colours and 'cool' bluish colours. Problems can arise when conventions conflict. For example, in a conventionally coloured relief map of the United States, the low-lying Death Valley in California will appear green, perhaps indicating to a user who associates green with forest or grassland that this is a fertile area!

Colour conventions have not been established for every kind of map and, as has been mentioned, some of them may conflict. It was in order to introduce some order into symbol design and the proper fitting of symbols to the features represented that Bertin developed his systematic approach. He considered that colour (i.e. hue) differences should be used only to indicate nominal (qualitative or categoric) differences among features. Lightness (value) differences could be used to indicate ordered and relative quantitative differences among features. So in a rainfall map made strictly according to Bertin's principles, the hue (blue) indicates water and a set of tints from light blue to dark blue indicate a sequence from low to high. Only by reference to the legend, however, can the user see exactly which rainfall class is represented by each tint.

As will be discussed in more detail in Chapter 7, Bertin's rules regarding colour and value can often not be applied strictly. Due to the nature of human vision, explained in Chapter 2, not all colours appear of equal value – for example in a rainbow the yellow colour band appears lighter than the red and blue bands. So differences in hue will automatically involve differences in value. In some cases this is done deliberately. Geological maps, for example, may contain dozens of different colours and the only way to ensure that they are sufficiently distinct from each other is to introduce differences in value. The converse situation arises in maps involving rather long value scales, for example a population density map with ten classes. If all these classes were represented by tints of one printing ink the user would have difficulty in comparing map colours to legend colours. To make the task easier, cartographers introduce a hue change, for example going from light yellow via orange to increasingly dark red. But there is a price to pay for this, at least for a paper map, and that is the introduction of at least one more printing ink.

A major drawback of Bertin's system as it applies to colour and value is that it ignores the third aspect of colour, namely its brilliance. Using more scientific terminology (Chapter 3) this is referred to as saturation or chroma. This aspect of colour can be introduced into the system as an additional variable. It has been used, perhaps subconsciously, by cartographers for many years, for example by placing very bright point symbols on dull background colours. Also, as will be shown in Chapter 3, making a tint of colour by adding white also decreases the saturation. The deliberate use of saturation as an independent colour variable has not perhaps achieved the attention it deserves, though some examples of its use are given in Chapter 7.

The influence of technical aspects

The more technical aspects of the production of colour on computer monitors and on paper are presented in Chapters 2, 3 and 5. Attention needs to be paid to these aspects at all times since they have a great influence on the appearance of the colours selected, especially when a coloured map or graphic is transferred from one medium to another.

In the early days of the use of colour on offset printed maps, every map colour required a separate printing plate. Topographic maps commonly required ten or eleven plates and geological maps perhaps more than fifty. Despite its cost and the time required, the great advantage of this system was that it could be standardised even using rather simple technology, provided the ink manufacturer kept the colours constant and the printer used the same paper and printing press. The method was very expensive for a few copies, but much cheaper per print for long printing runs. It was therefore ideally suited to producing many copies of a standard map series or an atlas. With the advent of percentage tint screens in large formats the number of printing plates could be reduced. For example, the light blue open water areas could be produced as a tint of the blue ink used for hydrographic linework and text. By overlaying tints of different inks, new colours could be produced. An example is orange produced by a tint of red on top of yellow. By these means the number of printing plates for a typical topographic map could be reduced from eleven or twelve to six or seven.

With some exceptions, maps in the days of analogue production methods consisted of solid colours and percentage tints. The production methods typically consisted of scribing, masking and applying photoset text. The exceptions involved printing continuously varying tints of a printing ink, a technique known as halftone screening. This was used for example in maps with relief shading or in photomaps, i.e. the combination of map symbols and text with aerial photographs. This was a much more complex process than using percentage tint screens and demanded skilled work by a photographer.

Skilled reproduction photographers were also required for the reproduction of coloured original images such as paintings or coloured photographs. This technique really developed commercially in the early years of the twentieth century, with the advent of process (or trichromatic) printing. It was found that by photographing an original through red, green and blue filters and printing negative halftone images in the colours cyan (C), magenta (M) and yellow (Y) respectively, a printed copy could be obtained that was very close in colour to the original. Usually black (K) was added, made from a photograph using no filter, in order to improve the final result (Figure 1.4). Great skill was, however, required at all stages of the procedure to get a good match with the original. Cartographers tended to avoid the method, preferring to stick to 'spot' colours, that is pre-mixed printing inks in exactly the colour required. The basic principles behind the process colour technique are explained in Chapter 2.

The production of all so-called screened images, whether percentage tints or halftone images in a single printing ink or the CMYK combination, has been completely revolutionised by the coming of the computer. The graphics industry was very quick

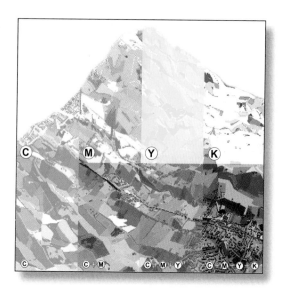

Figure 1.4 Separated CMYK colours and the combined results in print

to realise the enormous savings in time and costs that could be achieved. Expensive equipment such as large reproduction cameras and vacuum frames and the costly materials involved were no longer needed. Computer operators could produce good results with a fraction of the training that the photographers and reproduction experts had undergone. As the new techniques developed, it became possible to combine all aspects of a graphic on a computer screen to obtain a 'WYSIWYG' image – 'What You See Is What You Get'. Due to rapidly increasing computer power it became possible to achieve these results even on personal computers. This digital revolution has 'democratised' the production of high quality graphics, so that with a relatively small expenditure on hardware and software even an amateur can obtain an acceptable result.

Yet in some ways this is a problem. In the old days the experts working in the graphics industry had complete control of the entire process and the end product. In addition to the technical experts there were also highly trained graphic designers. The result was maps and atlases produced to a high standard in both aspects. Nowadays a technically high standard can be achieved fairly easily but many of the people producing graphics have had no formal design training, and this shows! This situation applies to many of those who use GIS software. They may be highly skilled in producing a geographical analysis but have little idea how to produce well-designed graphic output. This book therefore includes not only a basic explanation of the basic principles of colour and colour reproduction in the computer age, but also some indication of how to use colour well in a graphic design (Chapter 7).

Another problem often met with by GIS experts who have no formal graphics arts training arises when a map or graphic has to be offset printed. An output file that produces an acceptable result on an inkjet printer may give big problems when sent as it is to a commercial printing company (Figure 1.5). The company may have difficulty reading the file and producing printing plates from it. Even if a print can be produced there may be problems with symbols, text and colour. GIS experts, then, need to know something about how to deal with this situation so this topic is discussed, briefly, in Chapter 5.

Figure 1.5 A map as it might appear on a screen (left), output on an inkjet printer (centre) and as an offset print (right).
Note: this figure uses simulated colours.

Chapter 2

Colour vision, pigments and primary colours

What is colour?

The perception of colour is a complex process involving a physical stimulus (electromagnetic radiation), the physiological reaction of the eye and the psychological reaction of the brain to the signals sent by the eye along the optic nerve to the brain. It is important to remember that the colours we perceive in fact exist only in our brains.

The physical stimulus for colour is what we call light. Visible light consists of a very small part of the total electromagnetic spectrum, but a part in which the sun emits a large portion of its energy. (White) sunlight is made up of light of different wavelengths. The visible range extends from approximately 400 nm (nm = nanometres = 10^{-9} m) to approximately 700 nm. Colours are associated with particular ranges of wavelength. Just outside the visible range we find the 'invisible' colours infrared and ultraviolet that cannot be detected by our eyes, only by special equipment. Figure 2.1 shows Newton's classic experiment, in which he passed a narrow beam of sunlight through a glass prism, to separate the visible wavelengths and display the spectrum.

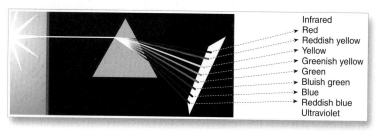

Infrared
Red
Reddish yellow
Yellow
Greenish yellow
Green
Bluish green
Blue
Reddish blue
Ultraviolet

Figure 2.1 Newton's classic experiment

Table 2.1 gives some indication of the colours we perceive and their respective wavelengths.

approximate wavelength (nm)	hue
380 - 470	reddish blue
470 - 475	blue
475 - 480	greenish blue
480 - 485	blue-green
485 - 495	bluish green
495 - 535	green
535 - 555	yellowish green
555 - 565	green-yellow
565 - 575	greenish yellow
575 - 580	yellow
580 - 585	reddish yellow
585 - 595	yellow-red
595 - 770	red

Table 2.1 Light wavelengths and the colours as we perceive them

The physiological reaction of the eye

The eye can be compared in some respects to a camera. Light passing through the pupil (diaphragm) is focused by a lens to form an image at the back of the eye, which is covered by millions of light sensitive cells forming the retina. When these cells are stimulated by light they send a signal via the optic nerve to the brain. There are two types of light sensitive cells, named rods and cones respectively. The rods are sensitive to very small amounts of light but do not lead to the sensation of colour in the brain. The cones are responsible for colour vision, but they need much larger amounts of light energy to be activated. This explains why our ability to see different colours decreases as night falls.

The human eye has three kinds of cones, each sensitive to a part of the visible light spectrum. The L-cones are sensitive mainly to long wavelengths, the M-cones to medium wavelengths and the S-cones to short wavelengths. The sensitivities of the different cone types overlap, as illustrated in Figure 2.2. There still appears to be some uncertainty about the exact shape of these sensitivity (or responsivity) curves. The figure, taken from some recent work by Shaw (1999) and in turn based on work by DeMarco, Pokorny and Smith (1992), shows the maximum responsivities of the S-, M- and L-cones to be at about 440 nm, 545 nm and 570 nm respectively. From the figure it can be seen that every

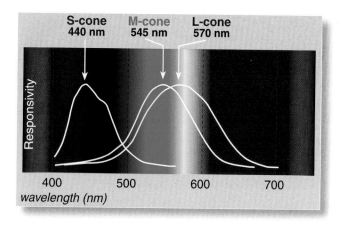

Figure 2.2 Spectral responsivity of the retinal cone cells (after Shaw, 1999)

single wavelength of the visible spectrum has associated with it a particular combination of stimulations of the three cone types. According to how much they are stimulated the cones send a neural message to the brain, which then 'creates' the appropriate colour. In the long wavelength part of the spectrum, where only the L-cones respond, the brain creates the colour we call red. In the central part of the spectrum, where the M-cones are stimulated more than the L-cones and where the S-cones have low responsivity, we see green. In the short wavelength part, where the S-cones have high responsivity and the other two cone types hardly respond, we see blue. Towards the short wavelength limit of perception the red cones retain some responsivity so we see a reddish blue, commonly called violet.

The colour yellow deserves a special mention here. This colour is seen in a narrow part of the spectrum in which the S-cones are not stimulated, the L-cones are at near maximum stimulation and the M-cones are somewhat less stimulated than the L-cones. Naturally occurring yellows, like flowers or ripe fruit, will normally reflect a broad spectrum of wavelengths in the medium and long wavelength regions. If this broad spectrum of wavelengths causes the cones to respond as they do for narrow-spectrum yellow then we will still see yellow. What matters for colour perception is not the actual wavelength composition of the light reaching the eye but the response of the cones. If all three cone types are stimulated equally we perceive white (for maximum stimulation), black (for very low stimulation) or grey (for intermediate stimulation).

Not all animals possess colour vision, and of those that do, not all possess three cone types. Many mammals, for example, have only two. One theory is that, in the primates (and thus in humans), one of the two cone types originally present gradually split into two as a result of evolution. This adaptation allowed, for example, yellow and red ripe fruit to be more easily distinguishable against the background of green leaves. This common origin would account for the high degree of overlap between the L-cones and the M-cones. It may also account for the commonest types of colour blindness, in which either the L-cones (protanopia) or the M-cones (deuteranopia) are missing. These two types of red-green colour blindness together affect about one in twenty human white males. White females and non-whites of both sexes are rarely affected. Cartographers tend to ignore the existence of colour blindness but if it is very important that all users be able to interpret a map correctly then the design should be checked by colour-blind persons.

Pigments and primary colours

Pigments are chemicals that have the property of absorbing some of the visible wavelengths. They are present within solid objects, liquids and gases, or they may be present only on the surface of an object, e.g. as a layer of paint or ink. The wavelengths that are not absorbed reach the eye by reflection if the pigment lies on or in an opaque surface or by transmission if the pigment is contained in a clear substance. Pigments therefore cause light from only a part of the complete visible spectrum to reach the eye. We could, for example, imagine dividing the complete spectrum at the points where the cone sensitivities overlap, i.e. at approximately 490 nm and 560 nm. By this means we can divide the spectrum into three parts, each part stimulating mainly one cone type. Light from a pigment that reflects or transmits only the long wavelength part stimulates mainly the L-cones. Correspondingly, the central part of the full spectrum stimulates mainly the M-cones and the short wavelengths stimulate mainly the S-cones. The three colours red(R), green(G) and blue(B) so created are called the primary colours. They are broad-spectrum colours, since each is composed of a broad region of the spectrum. It is also possible to use monochromatic primaries, each one reflecting or transmitting a single wavelength that stimulates one of the cone types much more than the other two. For example, the CIE colour matching system uses primaries with wavelengths 700 nm, 546.1 nm and 435.8 nm (Luo, 1998). What is important is not so much the spectral composition of the pigments but the stimulation of the cones. Note, however, that in the practical world outside the laboratory no existing pigments will reflect or transmit light to correspond exactly to what we desire – they will always reflect or transmit light of 'undesired' wavelengths and they may also partially absorb some wavelengths they are supposed completely to reflect or transmit. The RGB pigments we use in practice, therefore, are not 'pure'.

If we place three transparent filters in the colours red, green and blue in three white light projectors the result is beams of red, green and blue light respectively. Where the three beams overlap, we are in fact stimulating all three cone types to the maximum extent, so we perceive the reflected light from that area to be white. Where only two light beams overlap, the reflected light is no longer white. Blue and green together produce cyan, blue and red produce magenta, while red and green produce yellow (Figure 2.3). By varying the intensity of the light from each projector, different colours can be created. This process is called additive colour mixing.

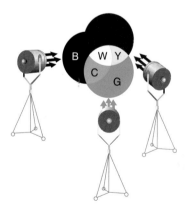

Figure 2.3 Additive colour mixing

An important application of additive colour mixing is colour television, or the colour monitor of a PC, using cathode ray tube (CRT) technology. Close examination of a television screen reveals tiny points of red, green and blue light, arranged in groups of three (Figure 2.4). All these points, which are actually phosphor dots, can independently vary in intensity. What can be perceived from a distance are not the single, individual dots, but the sum of the light they emit from an area. Colour monitors are described in some detail in Chapter 5 of this book.

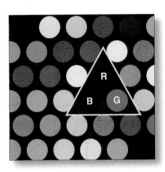

Figure 2.4 Red, Green and Blue phosphor dots on a colour monitor

Before leaving the topic of additive colour mixing, the colour yellow is worth mentioning again. As can be seen from Figure 2.2, yellow is created in the brain by a single wavelength of light of about 575 nm. It can also be created by mixing appropriate amounts of the R and G primaries. Our eyes do not therefore give us reliable information about the spectral composition of the light reaching them and it is possible for two colours to appear the same but to have different spectral compositions. Note that the fact that we perceive yellow as a distinct colour (it does not look like a mixture of red and green) is due to processes that take place in the brain.

Coloured illumination

How do colours in the world arise? Some of them are caused by refraction, like a rainbow, the blue sky or a soap bubble. Most colours, however, are due to the presence of pigments in liquids or transparent objects or in or on the surface of opaque objects. If, unusually, the illuminating light is itself coloured, the perceived colour of a pigment will change. For example a green object in red light appears black, or red writing on white paper seems to disappear in red light, since both reflect red.

For the paper map maker this has two important consequences.
1. Take care that the colours are still visible and distinct under artificial light, that is often not perfect white.
2. Test in actual use the colour distinctiveness on maps such as nautical and aeronautical charts that are used under special lighting conditions.

Subtractive colour mixing, the theory behind trichromatic printing

Coloured inks and paints can be obtained as either transparent or opaque liquids. In the case of transparent ink printed on white paper, the illuminating light passes through the ink and is reflected by the paper back through the ink layer. The reflected colour will be the colour of the transparent ink. If the paper itself is coloured the reflected colour will change, since the paper will absorb some wavelengths. If two or more layers of transparent ink are overprinted, each layer absorbs some of the light passing through it, so the result is different from the colours of the individual inks. If the printing ink is opaque the light reflects from the surface. The reflected colour will then always be the colour of the ink, regardless of the colour of the paper or of any underlying ink layer.

If we take transparent inks in the primary colours red, green and blue, and print any one of these over any other, the result is in theory black, since no light should pass through the combination and therefore no light can be reflected (Figure 2.5). In practice, due to the pigments not being 'pure' the combination would

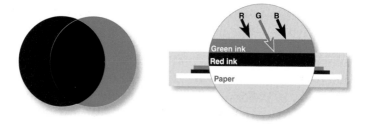

Figure 2.5 How green printed on top of red delivers black

reflect some light and, in the case of red on green, is likely to appear dark brown. Nevertheless we certainly cannot create light colours such as yellow by this means, as in additive mixing. It is, however, possible to get over this problem by using transparent inks in the colours cyan(C), magenta(M) and yellow(Y). Cyan ink transmits (primary) green and blue, magenta transmits red and blue, while yellow transmits red and green.

As an example let us take yellow ink printed on top of cyan ink on white paper and illuminated by white light (Figure 2.6). The yellow ink absorbs blue light and transmits only red and green. The cyan layer underneath now absorbs red light. So only the green light reaches the paper to be reflected back to the observer. The same result occurs if cyan ink is printed on top of yellow ink. In a similar way cyan and magenta produce blue and magenta and yellow produce red. This method of overprinting this set of transparent inks is called the subtractive or trichromatic system and is widely used in offset printing. It is also the basis of the colour printers used for computer output (Chapter 5).

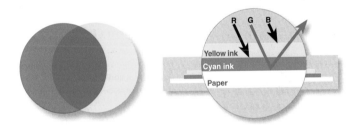

Figure 2.6 How cyan and yellow make green

The colours CMY are often called the subtractive primaries, or process colours. Note here, however, that yet again we come up against the problem that the pigments are in practice not completely 'pure'. Because they do not absorb and transmit 100% of the wavelengths expected in theory, each of these pigments appears to contain a certain amount of the other two. For this reason, cyan on top of magenta on top of yellow appears to be a dark brown instead of the expected black. It is normal therefore to add black(K) as a fourth printing colour. K refers to 'key', since in offset printing black is normally printed first and the other colours keyed or registered to the black image, which very often also contains most of the linework.

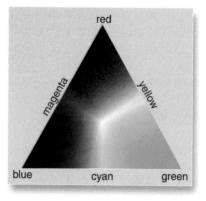

Figure 2.7 The colour triangle

The relationship between the additive and subtractive primaries is illustrated by the colour triangle (Figure 2.7). The colours on the sides of the triangles combine subtractively to produce the colours between them (Table 2.2), while the colours at the corners combine additively to produce the colours between them (Table 2.3).

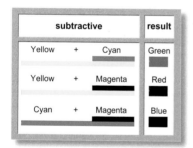

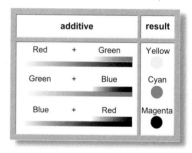

Table 2.2 Subtractive mixing   *Table 2.3 Additive mixing*

Note that in the triangle red, for example, is opposite cyan. These two mixed together additively will give white, mixed subtractively they will give black. Any two colours with this property are called complementary colours.

Let us consider that instead of printing solid colours we print screen tints, that is tiny dots of the colours (see also Chapter 5).

From a normal reading distance these dots will give the impression of a tint. The relative area covered by the dots is expressed as a percentage. Depending on the printing system, one may vary the size of the dots (most often applied in offset printing) or their spacing (as applied in inkjet printers). If we print a 30% tint of yellow on top of a 30% tint of cyan, the light reaching our eyes will be a mixture of yellow, cyan, green (where yellow dots overlap cyan dots) and white paper. The result will appear to be a light green (Figure 2.8).

By overprinting the subtractive primary colours cyan, magenta and yellow in different percentages it is possible to produce a great many colours. The ITC colour chart is an application of this system and shows the results of overprinting different percentage tints of the primary colours (Chapter 6).

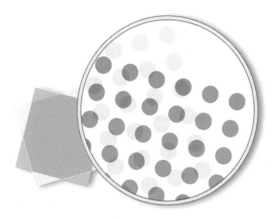

Figure 2.8 Tints of yellow and cyan produce light green

Mixed inks (spot colours)

The trichromatic printing system cannot reproduce all possible colours. Especially very brilliant colours may lie outside the range or gamut of producible colours. This is partly due to the fact that, as mentioned earlier, the available pigments for cyan, magenta and yellow are themselves not completely 'pure'. Another problem is that very pale colours cannot be achieved using the trichromatic system, since there is a lower limit to the size of the dots in offset printing and, in the case of inkjet printers, the dots of ink have to be spaced so far apart that smooth pale colours cannot be produced.

The use of dots causes other difficulties. For example, if we have to print a brown contour line using the trichromatic system, this line must be composed by overprinting three (screened) lines in the primary colours yellow, magenta and cyan. The resulting line will never be sharp, due to the technical difficulty of fitting the thin lines exactly on top of each other, and due to the fact that each line is in fact composed of dots.

Because of this it may be better to mix the inks themselves in liquid form and then to use this mixed ink for the actual offset printing which, in the example of contours, would consist of thin solid brown lines. Mixing inks is a job for a specialist. To achieve a specific colour it is necessary to mix some combination of yellow, magenta, cyan, red, green, blue and other colours, including black and white inks, in carefully controlled amounts. These pre-mixed colours are called spot colours. Although some national map agencies produce their maps using the trichromatic system, most topographic maps are printed using spot colours, often totalling six, including black. These spot colours may also be printed as percentage tints, for example open water as a tint of the blue used for streams. Percentage tints of two or three spot colours may be overprinted, for example 50% red on top of 100% yellow to produce orange. Geological maps may require ten or more spot colours, but nowadays, in order to reduce costs, standard trichromatic printing is becoming more popular here also, sometimes with the addition of a few spot colours.

All printing ink manufacturers supply a range of spot colours. One well known system is produced by the Pantone company (URL 2.1). All the Pantone colours are made by liquid mixing of any two or three of a basic set of nine coloured inks plus black and white in predetermined ratios. Pantone has become an accepted worldwide standard to specify colours and many printing ink manufacturers have a licence to manufacture the basic Pantone colours. Printers in Harare or in Singapore will understand exactly what colour you have in mind and be able to make it if that colour is specified according to the Pantone standard.

Nowadays most graphic images are created on digital systems. A major difficulty is that you may wish to match the spot colours of the design using the RGB of a monitor or the CMYK of a printer. An exact match can rarely be achieved even using the colour tables provided by manufacturers such as Pantone. One reason is, as mentioned above, that spot colour pigments exist that are outside the range (or gamut) of the colours that can be produced by standard additive or subtractive mixing. Another reason is that much depends on the colour characteristics of the CRT screen display or printer used and, in the case of the CRT screen, how well it is calibrated. A third reason, applicable to printed copies and explained above, is that very pale colours cannot be achieved.

The hexachrome system has been introduced to alleviate this situation in the case of subtractive colour mixing. Two extra printing colours, for example a pale magenta and a pale cyan, are added to the standard CMYK. Inkjet printers using this system are more expensive but produce very high quality colour output. The hexachrome system can also be used in offset printing. Pantone, for example, manufactures a hexachrome ink set (high chroma CMYK plus Hexachrome Orange and Hexachrome Green) that is guaranteed able to produce matches for 90% of the Pantone colours. This is double the amount that can be produced using CMYK only (URL 2.2).

Chapter 3

Colour description and colour spaces

The difficulty of describing colour

As was shown in the previous chapter, colour perception has a
physical cause (electromagnetic radiation of particular wavelengths)
leading to a physiological reaction in the eye that results in signals
travelling up the optic nerve to the brain. It is only in the brain that
what we know as 'colour' is created. This leads to the fundamental
problem that none of us can be absolutely certain that he or she
perceives exactly the same colours as somebody else when looking
at the same scene. We learn to describe as 'green' a colour that
other people also describe as 'green', but we cannot be sure that it
is the same green. Even colour-blind people may learn to use colour
names correctly for several colours, although it is certain that the
signals sent to their brains are different from those of people with
normal colour vision.

Notwithstanding this uncertainty, many experiments carried out
over the years have shown that people with normal colour vision
do not differ much in their colour perception. This leads to the
concept of the 'average' or 'standard' observer when discussing
colour perception. Several systems for colour description, such
as the Munsell system and the colour spaces defined by the CIE
(Commission Internationale de l'Eclairage, or, in English, the
International Commission on Illumination) are based on standard
observers. These systems are described later in this chapter.

A major difficulty when trying to describe colour is that our
language is not precise enough even when we try to be. If you
were to ask a roomful of people to go into town and come back
with a pot of 'medium light reddish brown' paint, the chances
are that no two would come back with exactly the same colour.
Artists have tried to get over this problem by giving special names
to colours, such as 'burnt sienna' or 'emerald green', but even these
are not totally precise. Scientists try to be exact so they are not

happy with these rather vague descriptions. Colour scientists have developed precise colour description systems based on the physical stimulation (light) and/or on the perception of the 'average' observer. A single, all-embracing system has not emerged, however. Depending on the intended use, some systems are more suitable than others. The situation is not unlike that of map projections, where different projections are needed for different uses.

With the advent of digital production systems in the graphics industry has grown the need for colour control at all stages of the production process, from inputting digital images and designing graphics on screen right through to the final result, often produced on a printing press. Cartography forms a part of the graphics industry and as such the standard production process is now also digital. Colour control in cartography can at its simplest consist of the use of a colour chart. This can be considered as a kind of colour description system, based as it is on a 'recipe' for the production of printed colours. The map designer selects colours from the chart and then does not care what they look like during all the production stages, being confident that at the final printed stage the colours will appear as desired. When the emphasis is on the exact reproduction of an original scene, object or piece of artwork, as is often the case in the commercial graphics industry, the graphics designers and production technicians prefer to use a colour management system that attempts as far as is possible to maintain constant colour throughout the entire production process. The basis of the technique is the use of mathematical models of colour.

Some definitions

The signals from the colour sensitive cells (cones), together with those from the rods (all with the same sensitivity, with a peak at just under 500 nm), are combined in the brain to give several different 'sensations' of colour. These sensations have been defined by the CIE (1989) in the 'International Lighting Vocabulary'.

> **Brightness:** the human sensation by which an area exhibits more or less light.
>
> **Hue:** the human sensation according to which an area appears to be similar to one, or to proportions of two, of the perceived colours red, yellow, green and blue.

Colourfulness: the human sensation according to which an area appears to exhibit more or less of its hue.

Lightness: the sensation of an area's brightness relative to a reference white in the scene.

Chroma: the colourfulness of an area relative to the brightness of a reference white.

Saturation: the colourfulness of an area relative to its brightness.

Note that the CIE definitions are not always used as carefully as they should be: for example brightness and lightness are often treated as if they are synonyms, as is also the case with chroma and saturation. Other terms, e.g. value and intensity, are in common use to describe aspects of colour. These terms are further explained and illustrated in the rest of this chapter.

The visual variables of colour

The design of cartographic symbols may be considered in terms of the graphic visual variables size, lightness (value), texture (grain), colour, orientation and form. The variable colour is not, however, a single variable: it can be expressed in terms of hue, lightness (or brightness) and colourfulness (expressed as saturation or chroma). These visual variables relate to how the brain processes the signals which reach it via the optic nerve from the eyes, and how the brain 'generates' the perceived colour. Any study of these variables has to be done therefore via human beings.

When we name a colour in everyday language we are really describing its **hue**. Purple is quite different in hue from green, for example (Figure 3.1). A particular hue results from a particular combination of different amounts of the visible light wavelengths. Some wavelengths will dominate, some may be absent altogether. A special case is the range of colours from white through a scale of grey to black. All of these have the characteristic that they reflect approximately equal amounts of all wavelengths – no

Figure 3.1 Different hues

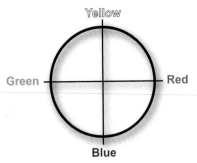

Figure 3.2 The opponent colour theory

particular wavelengths are dominant. These colours are in fact 'hue-less', or in more technical language, achromatic.

Hering (1964) developed in the late nineteenth century the now widely accepted opponent process theory of colour, based on how the brain interprets the signals coming from the retinal cone cells. His idea was that you can never describe a hue as both reddish and greenish, nor as both yellowish and bluish. These four basic hues can be arranged in a circle (Figure 3.2) with red opposite green and yellow opposite blue. We can envisage many hues falling between adjacent hues in the circle but no mixtures across the circle. For example we can imagine a whole series of purples between red and blue, but we cannot envisage any of these purples as containing yellow or green. The idea of a colour circle or colour wheel was not of course new, being used among others by Goethe in his studies of colour, but what was new was the scientific explanation. Hering maintained that the sensation of 'redness' or 'greenness' arises when the brain compares the signals from the L and M cones (Chapter 2), while 'yellowness' or 'blueness' arises when the brain compares the signals from the S cones to the sum of the signals from the L and M cones. Hue circles of various types are fundamental to many systems for describing colour.

The variable *lightness* may also be called value. The best way to think about lightness is to consider a black and white photograph of a coloured scene. On the photo, the only colour variable present is lightness. English language words like 'light' and 'dark' refer to the variable lightness (Figure 3.3).

Figure 3.3 Variation in lightness

In this way, colours may have the same hue but differ in lightness (light red and dark red, for example). The corollary of this is that for any colour a grey can be found that has the same lightness as that colour. Because of the varying total sensitivity of the eye to different wavelengths (it is most sensitive around the middle of the visual range) there is no direct relationship between the amount of light energy reaching the eye and the sensation of lightness. A given amount of energy in the yellow region of the spectrum will result in a much lighter apparent colour than the same energy at the red or blue end of the spectrum. Normal panchromatic black and white photographic film is designed to react very much like the human eye in this respect, so that for example yellows on a black and white photograph appear lighter than reds.

Furthermore, lightness is a relative concept. If you take a black and white photograph and put it under a strong lamp the amount of reflected energy increases, i.e. the brightness of all the greys increases in proportion, yet the relative lightness appears to stay the same. The situation is different in the case of a monitor. If you shine a lamp on a monitor the reflected light is added to the light emitted by the monitor. This causes the relative differences in brightness in the screen image to decrease so that the lightness differences decrease also: the image on the screen appears to lose contrast. For this reason it is always best when working with a monitor to try to keep the ambient light constant and to avoid light shining directly on to the screen.

The variable **saturation** (or chroma) may be a more difficult concept to understand. It describes the purity of a colour. 'Vivid' and 'dull' are examples of common English language words used to describe colours of high and low saturation respectively. If you take a colour of high purity and a grey of the same lightness, and mix them as liquids in different proportions, you are in fact creating a chroma scale with the pure colour at one end and the grey at the other (Figure 3.4). It is worth noting here that adding

Figure 3.4 A chroma scale

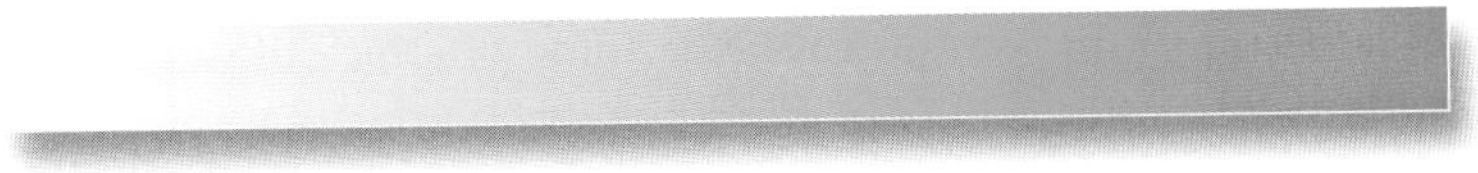

Figure 3.5 A tint scale

white to a colour (to make a tint) makes it lighter but also decreases its saturation (Figure 3.5). The same applies to the percentage tints referred to in Chapter2.

Some commercial colour libraries

Several commercial companies have developed their own systems for describing and encoding colour. Most attempt to place colours in some kind of logical sequence, but the approach is not truly scientific. These colour systems are designed for use for offset printing, and are therefore difficult to transfer to the additive mixing of a RGB display screen.

Pantone is perhaps the most widely used of these commercial systems. Each colour in the system is created by the mixing

Libary name	Type	Description
Dainippon	spot	Colours are organised into three categories: gay/brilliant quiet/dark greys, metallic
Focoltone	spot	A range of spot colours built from the process colours
Toyo	spot	Similar to Pantone but uses 11 basic colours
Trumatch	process-colours	Specified in small CMYK increments to avoid colour gaps

Table 3.1 Some colour libraries

together of coloured inks in given proportions, usually with the addition of black and/or white. The colours are selected from a small basic set. Because the system is so widely used in the graphics industry it is available as a colour library in many Desk Top Publishing (DTP) programs, being imitated by the additive mixture of RGB on the monitor.

In addition to the Pantone system, some graphic software programs also offer other standard colour libraries that were originally developed for the printing industry (Table 3.1)

Colour names

As was mentioned at the beginning of this chapter, language is very imprecise when it comes to naming colours. Furthermore, some languages have very few basic colour names. For those that are well developed in this respect, research has shown (Berlin and Kay, 1969) that there are eleven basic colour terms in general use, denoted in English by the colour names black, white, grey, red, green, yellow, blue, brown, purple (or violet), orange and pink. This high level of agreement probably has its origins in the physiology of human colour vision.

Some of the common colour names are more precise than others: for example, there will be no argument about what is 'black' or 'white', but a rather large number of colours will be called 'brown' by at least some people. Many descriptive words and special terms have been introduced by artists, technicians and others over the centuries to try to describe colour more exactly. Yet there is no complete agreement about even the more modern words like 'magenta' that are supposed to be precise.

Facing this difficulty, the American National Bureau of Standards (NBS) requested the Inter-Society Color Council (ISCC) to classify colour names. This resulted in 1955 in the NBS/ISCC colour naming system. It uses the basic colour names mentioned above to describe the hue aspect of a colour (with purple and violet as different hues) and adds the name 'olive'. All hues are described by these names or various combinations, e.g. 'yellowish green', 'yellow-green', 'greenish yellow', resulting in 26 hue names, plus white, grey and black [URL 3.1].

Each hue is then modified using a standard vocabulary, consisting of the words light, medium, dark, pale, moderate, brilliant, strong, deep and vivid. For each hue the modifiers are arranged in two dimensions corresponding to the visual variables lightness and chroma so that the colours go from black (dark) to white (pale or light) in the Y direction and from grey to vivid in the X direction (Figure 3.6).

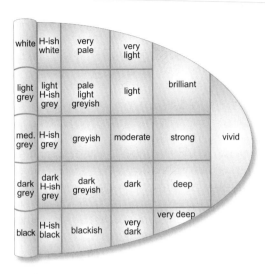

Figure 3.6 A typical NBS/ISCC colour naming system arrangement, for hue H

Assuming that lightness and chroma are continuous variables, there are in fact no sharp boundaries between adjacent colours in this arrangement. The so-called centroid colours, however, are sufficiently far apart to be perceived as distinct colours by the 'average' observer. Not every hue has its full complement of modifiers because of non-linearities in our perception of colour and irregularities in our natural-language system of colour names. The resulting system has in fact only 267 centroid colours.

The arrangement of colours in the NBS/ISCC system is very similar to the arrangement of colours in the Munsell system described below. All the NBS/ISCC colours have in fact been given Munsell codes. They have also been translated into their RGB equivalents for display on computer monitors [URL 3.2]. Note, however, that on a given computer system the RGB colours will frequently not correspond exactly to the original NBS/ISCC colours and the same RGB colour may appear very different on different computer systems, for example PC and Apple.

Colour spaces

A colour space is a method, based on scientific principles, by which we can specify, create and visualise colour. As humans, we may define a colour by its attributes of brightness, hue and colourfulness. A computer may describe a colour using the amount (often referred to as intensity) of red, green and blue phosphor emission required to match a colour. A printing press may produce a specific colour in terms of the reflectance and absorption of cyan, magenta, yellow and black inks on the printing paper.

A colour can be specified in three-dimensional space by using three coordinates, or parameters. These parameters describe the position of the colour within the colour space being used. It is very important, however, to realise that there are different colour spaces for different purposes, so the same colour will have different parameters in different spaces. Some of these spaces are based on physically measuring the spectral power distribution of a colour and then converting to three parameters, some are based on the amount of RGB (or CMY), while others are based on the mixing of a basic set of liquid pigments and letting the 'standard' observer judge the results. This is a little like geographic referencing, where the same position on the Earth's surface will have a different grid reference depending on the projection and related grid being used.

Just as in the case of map projections, different colour spaces are better for different applications. Some colour spaces are perceptually linear, i.e. a 10-unit change in stimulus will produce the same change in perception wherever it is applied. Many colour spaces, particularly those used in computer graphics, are conceptually rather simple but not linear in this way. Some colour spaces are intuitive to use, i.e. it is easy for the user to navigate within them and to create desired colours. Finally, some colour spaces are device dependent while others are so-called device independent. Transforming colour specifications from one colour space to another is one of the main practical problems encountered when using colour. This is especially true when transferring from a colour monitor to paper.

Some colour spaces used for surface colours

As discussed above, one of the problems in the use of colour is how to describe the required colour. To avoid this problem many colour order systems have been devised to give a more systematic approach to describing colour, by providing a set of colours to use for matching reflected (surface) colours. The general principle is the same in most of these. Hues are arranged in a circle, saturation (or chroma) increases outward from the centre, and perpendicular to the centre runs the achromatic axis from black to white. The most highly saturated obtainable examples of the different hues are then mixed with different amounts of black and white pigments, as liquids, and applied to a surface, usually white paper, that is then viewed under a standard white light source. The resulting colours are arranged systematically according to the rules of the particular system and the final colour solid is cut or dissected in some way for display on a flat surface. The systems can be divided into two main groups, those that give a symmetrical shape and those where the shape of the colour solid is not symmetrical. An early example of a symmetrical colour solid is the Ostwald system.

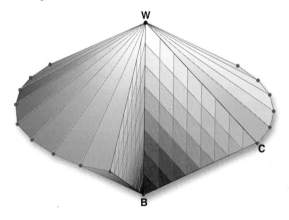

Figure 3.7 The Ostwald colour system

The Ostwald system dates from 1916 (Figure 3.7 and URL 3.3). The hues are arranged in a circle with opposite hues complementary. In the original version there were 24 hues. The central axis contains the achromatic colours, with black at the bottom and white at the top. For each hue there are 28 colours (in the abbreviated version of the original system), each colour variation being a mixture of the 'pure' hue plus black and white. The total number of colours in the system is therefore 680, including the 8-step achromatic scale from black to white. For all mixtures of colours, hue content plus white content plus black content equals 1. Ostwald did not use terms like chroma and lightness in his system, but in general you can say that chroma increases outwards from the central axis and lightness increases upwards in the solid, that has a double cone shape like a spinning top.

In the symmetrical Ostwald system all the high chroma colours lie in a circle, located midway up the solid. We have seen already, however, that high chroma colours do not appear to have the same lightness. In the Ostwald system a horizontal plane through the system therefore does not contain colours of equal lightness, which is the case in the Munsell system described below. Another major disadvantage of the Ostwald system is that it is a closed system that does not allow the addition of more saturated colours as new pigments are discovered.

Because of its simple, symmetrical structure the Ostwald system can easily be adapted to the trichromatic system, using mathematical formulae for either additive or subtractive primaries. Several colour spaces used in computer graphics and described later in this chapter are very similar to the Ostwald system. The ITC colour chart is also similar to this system.

The ideas of Ostwald and of Hering have been combined in the Natural Colour System (NCS), much used in Scandinavia (Figures 3.8, 3.9 and URL 3.4). The hue circle is based on the opponent pairs R-G and B-Y. All other hues can be defined in terms of their apparent mixture of two adjacent main hues, i.e. R with Y, Y with G, G with B and B with R. The complete colour solid is a double cone, like the Ostwald system, with the central axis running from black at the bottom to white at the top. All colours in the solid then have a hue component (C) plus a whiteness (W) and a blackness (S) component. The total of all three is always 100. The greys of the central axis have of course hue component zero.

One of the best known asymmetrical colour order systems is that developed by Munsell at about the same period as Ostwald early in the twentieth century, but still accepted as a standard [URL 3.5]. It is based upon the variables hue, value and chroma applied to a three-dimensional colour solid, as shown in Figure 3.10.

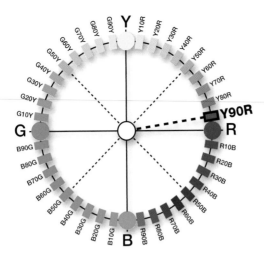

Figure 3.8 The hue circle of the Natural Colour System (NCS)

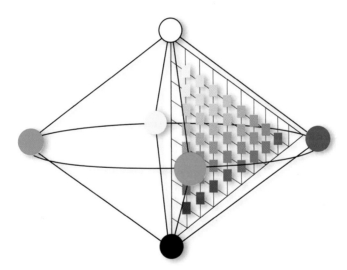

Figure 3.9 The NCS colour space

Hues are arranged in a circle, chroma increases outward from the central axis containing the achromatic colours, and value increases upward from black at the bottom to white at the top. The Munsell hues are made by first arranging five basic hues in a circle, then mixing adjacent hues in different proportions. The

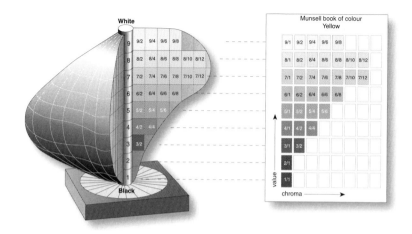

Figure 3.10 The three-dimensional colour solid of the Munsell system. A quarter of the solid is removed to show the interior arrangement

original system contains a circle of 100 hues, but a reduced version with only forty hues is commonly used as well. The variations in value and chroma are produced by adding white and black in different proportions.

The central axis of the system is a grey scale. Munsell chose grey values so that the steps in the scale appear perceptually equal from 0 (theoretically perfect black) to 10 (theoretically perfect white). He did not simply use equal differences in the amount of light reflected. This is because the response of the eye is nonlinear: it is roughly logarithmic. As the amount of light energy increases, a larger stimulation difference is required to produce the same perceptual difference (Figure 3.11).

Munsell made his grey scale after experimentation on many human subjects. He did the same with the chroma and hue scales, to achieve perceptually equal steps. The colour space as a whole is not perceptually linear, however, since the perceptual difference between adjacent hues becomes less towards the central axis. It can be seen from Figure 3.10 that the Munsell solid is neither a cylinder nor a double cone. The solid narrows towards the central axis at the black and white ends. This is because black and white, being achromatic colours, have zero chroma, therefore colours close to black and white must have

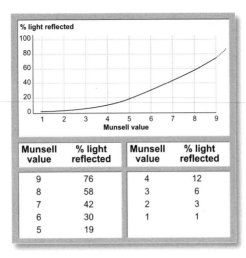

Munsell value	% light reflected	Munsell value	% light reflected
9	76	4	12
8	58	3	6
7	42	2	3
6	30	1	1
5	19		

Figure 3.11 Munsell's grey scale

low chroma. The solid is not symmetric because the eye is not uniformly sensitive to all hues.

Yellow appears lighter than purple even if the two are reflecting equal amounts of light energy. In the Munsell system, therefore, a high chroma yellow will be placed higher on the value scale than a high chroma purple.

In the system a simple coding system gives every colour square a unique code. The Munsell system is available from licensed producers in book form. Each page of the book contains all the colour variations of a single hue. Because every colour has to be mixed and printed individually, then cut in rectangles and stuck on to the page, the book is very expensive. Smaller, much cheaper versions with only some hues are produced for example for soil scientists, who can then describe a soil colour accurately by finding the closest match in the book. The Munsell system is available (transferred to RGB and therefore of lower accuracy) as a colour library in some DTP graphics packages. It can be studied in RGB form in a small computer program that, in a beta version, was downloadable in mid-2001 from the Munsell website [URL 3.6]. The Munsell colours are also to be found on colour research websites, such as URL 3.7.

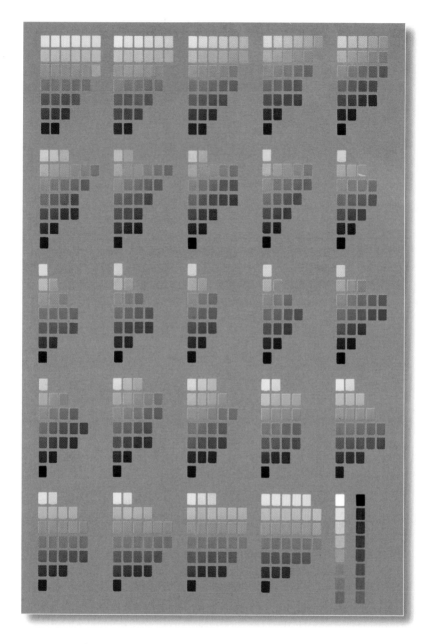

Figure 3.12 The DIN 6164 colours (simulated using CMYK). Copyright Muster-Schmidt, Göttingen.

As mentioned earlier, the arrangement of colours in the NBS/ISCC colour naming system is very similar to that of Munsell. Some other colour order systems that were developed after Munsell did his work are also very similar. An example is the German standard, DIN 6164, produced by the 'Deutsches Institut für Normung'. The initiative for a system to replace the Ostwald system in that country arose in the 1930s but the final results of the research team led by Manfred Richter were not published until 1953 [URL 3.8]. The idea was to create a system using the variables of hue, saturation (or chroma) and brightness that would be as perceptually equidistant as possible. The hue circle consists of 24 'equidistant' hues beginning at yellow (1) and proceeding via red (7), blue (16) and green (22) back to yellow. In this system opposite hues are not exact complementaries and neither is red opposite to green nor yellow opposite to blue. In the DIN system hue is represented by T, saturation by S (on a scale from 0 to 6) and darkness by D (with 10 as ideal black and 0 for ideal white and all optimal colours). It is the notion of 'darkness' that mainly distinguishes DIN 6164 from Munsell. This is a complex idea, perhaps best explained as a measure of the amount of black that appears to be present in a colour. A horizontal plane through the DIN 6164 solid, therefore, does not contain colours of constant Munsell value. Nevertheless, the solid is asymmetrical and not unlike the Munsell solid. The arrangement of the 588 colours of DIN 6164, including the grey scale, is shown in Figure 3.12. The colours are here reproduced using CMYK so they are of course not accurate.

The colour order systems described briefly here are only a sample of many. All of them are, however, based on the same principle, the mixture in liquid pigment form of highly saturated colours with black and white. Most colours in one system will therefore have a perfect or at least a close match to colours in any of the others: all that differs is the code number.

The cubical colour space based on RGB or CMY

All the colours produced by additive mixing on a colour monitor can be expressed in terms of the amount of RGB. These numerical values can then be plotted along three axes to create a cube (Figure 3.13). The corner of the cube where RGB are

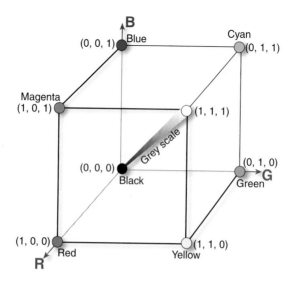

Figure 3.13 The RGB colour cube

all zero represents black, the corner where they are all at full intensity (let us say 1) represents white. The other six corners are R, G, B, C, M, Y.

The same cube can be used to represent subtractive mixtures of CMY. In this case zero CMY represents the white of the paper, while full (i.e. 1) CMY represents black. The two sets of axes have a very simple mathematical relationship to each other. If we now consider the proportions of R, G and B, or of C, M and Y present in a colour, then $R = 1 - C$, $G = 1 - M$ and $B = 1 - Y$.

This seems to be a very simple, attractive colour space, and it is in fact much used. It has many disadvantages, however. The main ones are listed below.

- The cube is not intuitive: there is no obvious relationship with the visual variables hue, lightness and saturation.
- The space is device dependent. Different monitors, and even an adjustment to the same monitor, will give different colours. The colours on a monitor are also very much affected by the ambient light. In the subtractive version there is also no standard result: offset printing will give a different result from inkjet printing, for example.

- There is a nonlinear relationship between the voltage supplied to the monitor and the intensity or brightness of the resulting light, which the CIE has defined in terms of luminance. Also, as mentioned earlier, human vision has a nonlinear perceptual response to brightness: a source having a luminance only 18% of a reference luminance appears about half as bright. The transfer functions that are used to create the image on the screen from digital data governing intensity (often on the scale 0–255) attempt to take account of these factors. Despite this, the scales along the RGB axes may not be entirely perceptually linear.
- If the cube is used in subtractive mode there is also nonlinearity: printed tints of CMY usually appear darker than expected (see also Chapter 6).
- If you desire a simple conversion from RGB to CMY, the first requirement is that all the corners of the cube appear to be the same colour in both systems. Yet this never happens. In the first place it is very difficult to match colours produced by emitted light (the additive system) to colours produced by reflected light (the subtractive system). In the second place the pigments RGB and CMY are never theoretically 'pure', and are therefore unlikely to be perfect complementary matches. Thirdly, even if you could somehow adjust the corners of the additive and the subtractive cubes to have the same colours, the nonlinearities in both systems do not correspond, so the simple transformation given above, e.g. $R = 1 - C$, would not be correct.

It is possible to find transformations to relate a given colour in a particular RGB cube to the same colour in a particular CMY cube but the equations are complex. The simple transformation given above will produce acceptable results if colours are used very simply and some change of colour in the printed result does not matter, as in business graphics. It is definitely not recommended for maps using many colours, such as geological maps.

HLS, HSV and related colour spaces
One of the problems that we have seen with the RGB or CMY cube is that the cubical space is not intuitive and not very practical in colour selection. It does not correspond to how we perceive colour. If, however, we take the cube and transform

it into a double cone, with black and white at the apexes and RGBCMY arranged in a circle in the sequence RYGCBM, we create a colour space that has many similarities to the Ostwald colour solid. The original idea for this space was based on the additive mixture of R, G and B and used the classic variables for additive mixture of hue (H), luminance (L) and saturation (S), so creating the HLS space. Often, somewhat confusingly, L is taken to mean lightness instead of luminance. There are several variations on this space, e.g. HSL, IHS (intensity, hue, saturation), HCI (hue, chroma, intensity) or HSB (hue, saturation, brightness). Figure 3.14 shows a HLS space as a hexacone.

A space like this is more intuitive than the cube. Hues are arranged in a circle, so any colours with the same direction from the central axis (constant hue angle) have in theory the same hue. Diametrically opposite colours have complementary hues. Saturation increases outwards from the central axis, and lightness

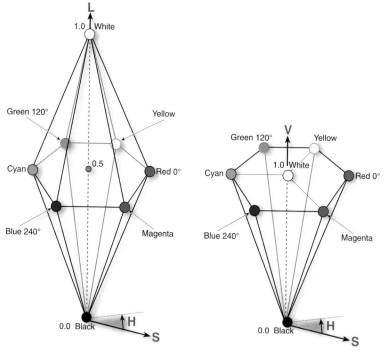

Figure 3.14 The HLS colour space   *Figure 3.15 The HSV colour space*

increases upwards. All of these characteristics make colour selection easier.

A double cone space also suffers from severe disadvantages, however.

- An Ostwald-type space is inherently perceptually nonlinear. Furthermore, the factors giving rise to nonlinearity in the cube also apply to this space. In addition, it should be noted that 'pure' R, G, B, C, M and Y on a CRT display do not have equal chroma (for an explanation see the next section, on CIE colour spaces).
- Like the colour cube, the space is device dependent, and suffers from the same problems when trying to convert from an additive space to a subtractive space.
- There is no universally accepted set of equations for converting the cube to the double cone. This has the result that coordinates in one system cannot be used directly in any other.
- The plane containing the colours of highest chroma has lightness 0.5, yet these colours do not appear to have the same lightness: high chroma yellow, for example, appears lighter than high chroma blue.
- The system introduces an arithmetic discontinuity at 360° for hues. This is not useful for image computation since you cannot perform arithmetic mixtures of colours expressed in polar coordinates.

A somewhat different colour space, the HSV space (hue, saturation, value), is based on a single cone (Figure 3.15). This is clearly even more nonlinear than the HLS space.

When these two colour spaces (or, more accurately, colour models) are used to define colours for display on a computer monitor they have to be based on the additive mixture of RGB. The equations for finding the values of HLS and HSV from given intensity levels of R, G and B are to be found in many sources, including Palus (1998). For both models, several equations for calculating H exist, depending on whether accuracy or computational simplicity is sought after. The geometrical differences between the two spaces arise from different methods of calculating S and L (or V).

Using 'max' and 'min' to represent the maximum and minimum values respectively of R, G and B,

In the HLS system:

L = (max + min)/2

    If L = 0, then S = 0

    If L ≤ 0.5, then S = (max − min)/(max + min)

    If L > 0.5, then S = (max − min)/(2 − max − min)

In the HSV system:

V = max

    If max = 0, then S = 0

    If max > 0, then S = (max − min)/max

In actual practice nowadays, the intensity levels of R, G and B on the computer screen are most often defined on the scale 0–255. The values of S, L and V are often also expressed on that scale. The two colour spaces HLS and HSV resulting from these calculations have intuitive value in that they appear to fit the perceptual visual variables. This appearance is deceptive, however. As mentioned earlier, the transfer functions used to create the screen image attempt to create a luminance scale that appears to give perceptually equidistant steps, for example on an intensity scale from 0 to 255, for each of R, G and B. The psychological variable lightness is, however, a relative concept and depends for its estimation on the existence of a reference white in the scene. The apparent lightness of R, G and B and their mixtures is therefore difficult to predict just from their luminance. Furthermore, the eye is most sensitive to wavelengths near the centre of the visible spectrum, so that G will appear lighter than R or B, for the same luminance. This is of course a difficulty with all symmetrical double-cone spaces.

    Something else to watch out for is that not all so-called HLS and HSV systems are calculated using the equations given above. For example, sometimes L is found by:

L = (R + G + B)/3

This has some logic behind it: magenta (R + B) has a higher luminance than just R or B. However, using this equation, full intensity R, G or B has L-value 0.33 (on the scale 0 to 1), while full intensity C, M or Y has L-value 0.67. These colours obviously do not lie on the 0.5 L-value plane.

Some GIS and graphics software packages use the HSV system, displayed graphically and numerically in an interactive colour selection window. With V set at maximum the colour circle is shown with white at the centre and the most saturated colours around the circumference. Any colour can be chosen by pointing the cursor somewhere in the circle, upon which the calculated values of H, S and V appear in the display. The operation can be performed in reverse by typing in the desired values. A slider bar alongside the circle is used to change the value for V, with black at the bottom and white at the top. As V becomes less the circle as a whole becomes darker. According to the HSV space shown in Figure 3.15 the colour circle should become smaller towards the black point. Usually, however, the circle size in the window remains unchanged, yet saturation remains measured by the distance from the centre. This is correct if saturation is considered to be a relative quantity but it does not correlate with chroma (Figure 3.16). An interactive HSV colour system can be downloaded from the efg website [URL 3.9].

Clearly, the HLS and HSV colour spaces are intrinsically not ideal and some rather purist colour scientists recommend that these simple colour spaces be abandoned. The problem is that users like them because, especially in the form of interactive colour circles, they appear to be so easy to handle. In actual fact the versions used in practice in software packages can be misleading, since lightness and saturation are usually not maintained as truly independent variables.

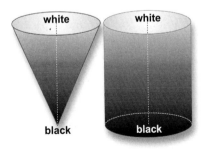

Figure 3.16 HSV as a cylinder instead of a cone

CIE colour spaces

In 1931 the CIE introduced a device-independent colour space called the XYZ colour system, which is still accepted as a standard for colour description [URL 3.10]. It is based on the characteristics of the human visual system. One of its main advantages is that, from physical measurements using a spectrophotometer, colours can be plotted on a two-dimensional graph derived from the space.

The system is based on the RGB primaries, although it uses artificial primaries, called tristimulus values. X represents red, Y represents green and Z represents blue. Each of these values is based on the sensitivity of the corresponding retinal cone type to different wavelengths. The sensitivity of the green cones in the eye is very close to the sensitivity of the eye as a whole to different wavelengths. The Y stimulus value is therefore also the luminance (the observed brightness) of the colour. Using complex equations any colour, i.e. any spectral power distribution, can be converted into tristimulus values.

In order to plot colours on a graph, the tristimulus values are converted into chromaticity coordinates x, y and z as follows:

$$x = X/(X + Y + Z)$$
$$y = Y/(X + Y + Z)$$
$$z = Z/(X + Y + Z)$$

You need to plot the x and y values only, since the z value can be found directly from the fact that $x + y + z = 1$. The graph is called the chromaticity diagram (Figure 3.17). The pure spectral colours of the rainbow are found on the outer curved line. The purples, which are mixtures of red and blue, are found along the line joining the red and blue ends of the spectrum. The reason that the graph is called the chromaticity diagram is that it shows only the relative amounts of the three primaries, which together determine what is called the chromaticity of a colour. To define a colour completely you also need to know the tristimulus value Y.

Besides being device independent, the chromaticity diagram is useful in other ways.

• It is reasonably intuitive. Direction determines hue, and complementary hues are diametrically opposite, through the

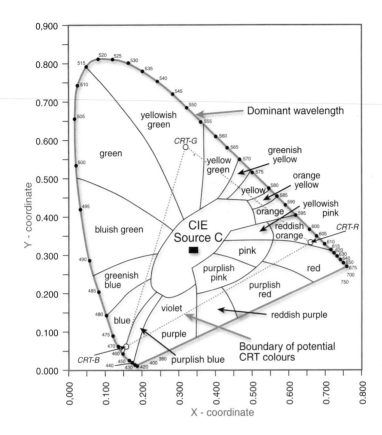

Figure 3.17 The CIE chromaticity diagram

'white point' ($x = y = z = 0.33$). The distance from the white point is an expression of chroma (more accurately the distance from the white point to the hue point relative to the distance from the white point through the hue point to the pure spectral line).

- The additive mixture of two colours in any proportion is found along the straight line connecting the two plotted colours. A corollary of this is that all colours formed by the additive mixture of any three colours are to be found within the triangle connecting them. This fact is much used by television engineers to express the 'colour gamut' of a CRT display. A typical set of

CRT primaries is plotted in Figure 3.17, together with the triangular gamut. It is worth noting here that the graph explains why cyan on a CRT display appears 'weak', i.e. of low saturation or chroma. The purest cyan is found midway along the line joining the blue and green primaries, which is rather close to the white point, hence the low chroma of cyan. On the other hand, the purest yellow, which is midway between red and green, has high chroma.

The CIE chromaticity diagram is perceptually nonlinear. As an attempt to solve this problem, the CIE carried out a transformation to this space in 1976 to create the Uniform Colour Space (Figure 3.18). In this space, equal measured distances are supposed to represent equal perceptual distances.

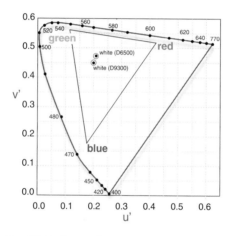

Figure 3.18 The CIE Uniform Colour Space

The main drawback of the chromaticity diagram is that luminance is not represented graphically but by a separate number, the Y tristimulus value. Many attempts have been made to add this value to a set of two-dimensional coordinates in order to create a three-dimensional colour space. The CIE itself has created two such spaces, CIELUV and CIELAB. For a more extended description of these than that given here see URL 3.11.

Figure 3.19 shows the CIELUV colour space recommended by the CIE for additive colour mixture, e.g. computer monitors. The coordinates are named L*, u* and v*. L* is derived from the Y

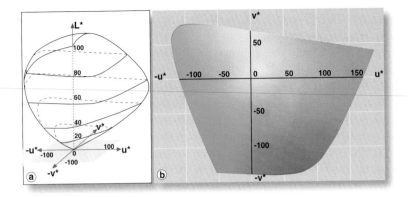

Figure 3.19 The CIELUV colour space

tristimulus value, and has minimum and maximum values 0 and 100 respectively. It takes into consideration the nonlinear relationship between lightness and luminance. u* and v* are orthogonal axes mainly derived from the chromaticity coordinates x and y. These axes cross at the white point. Figure 3.19(a) shows the three-dimensional solid, and Figure 3.19(b) shows a horizontal cross-section at the level L* = 50. The CIELUV space uses linear transformations from the original CIE XYZ system, so retaining the basic properties of this system. It is widely used by television engineers.

The CIELAB colour space (Figure 3.20) uses different transformations from those of the CIELUV space. Like it, L* is derived from the Y tristimulus values. The other two axes, a* and b*, are expressions of what is called the opponent colour theory of colour vision referred to earlier. In the CIELAB space, −a* is green and +a* is red, −b* is blue and +b* is yellow. The two axes cross at the white point. Note, however, that the a* and b* axes are derived from the XYZ values and do not correspond exactly to the red-green and yellow-blue axes as found by Hering. Figure 3.20(a) shows the three-dimensional solid, Figure 3.20(b) shows a horizontal cross-section at the level L* = 50.

The values of a* and b* are derived by means of nonlinear transformations from the tristimulus values. Because of this nonlinearity, the CIELAB space has no associated two-dimensional chromaticity diagram and no correlate for saturation. This colour space has, however, become accepted as a standard for

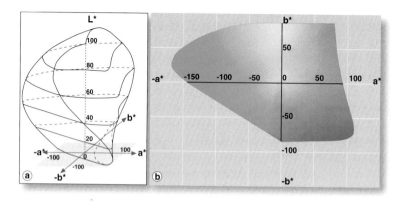

Figure 3.20 The CIELAB colour space

applications involving surface colours (reflected light) and is used in the graphics industry for colour management systems, dealt with in more detail in Chapter 5.

Colour gamut

Colour order systems such as Munsell and Ostwald and colour models such as HLS and HSV contain colours achievable by using a set of pigments. The range of achievable colours in each case is called the colour gamut. Not all the colours achievable in one system, however, may be achievable in another: their gamuts differ. Furthermore, extremely saturated colours and the monochromatic colours of the rainbow cannot be achieved by any colour system based on pigments.

The CIE systems are based on colours achievable in a laboratory situation. They are bounded by the monochromatic colours of the rainbow at maximum chroma. In other words, all possible colours can be plotted in these systems. Figures 3.19 and 3.20 are actually misleading in the sense that the printing colours used to print this book cannot reproduce the colours near the outer boundary of these colour spaces.

Colour gamut is not only a property of colour order systems and of colour models but also of input devices such as scanners, dealt with in the next chapter, and of output devices, described in Chapter 5. Figure 3.21 shows some typical gamuts plotted on the CIE chromaticity diagram. The diagram shows significant differences among the colour gamuts for colours of high chroma.

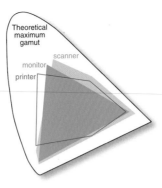

Figure 3.21 The differences in colour gamut of input and output devices

Within each type of device there are also differences. Furthermore, gamuts can change with the age of a device. This is particularly true of colour monitors.

It is also possible to plot gamuts on one of the CIE colour spaces. Figure 3.22 shows two aspects of the colour gamut of a typical thermal sublimation printer, plotted on the CIELAB colour space. The diagrams are in fact taken from a website containing virtual reality views of several colour gamuts [URL 3.12]. The original colour cube becomes distorted of course after plotting in this space.

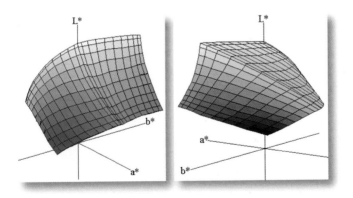

Figure 3.22 Two views of the colour gamut of a thermal sublimation printer (source: URL 3.12). Copyright Dr. P. Herzog.

Chapter 4

Colour input

Raster image data

Before discussing colour output, it seems logical to deal
with colour input, in particular the input of data into a GIS.
Mostly the data will consist of vectors (Figure 4.1a) giving
the position of spatial objects and attribute tables containing
information on them. But part of the information can be a raster
file of an image, either satellite imagery, an aerial photograph, a
hill shading derived from a digital elevation model (Figure 4.1b),
a scanned paper map or a picture of an object to be displayed
or attached to an element in the final map. The type of files to
be treated in this section is the raster type. Vector data are,
in this case, not of interest, since colours are attached to
vectors only during the final visualisation stage and not
during input.

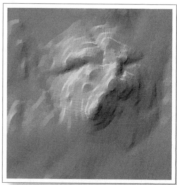

Figure 4.1a Vector contour lines   *Figure 4.1b A raster image – hill shading*

A digital raster image is usually taken from the real world via a digital camera, from an analogue image via a scanner or grabbed from the monitor. A raster image is composed of pixels (a contraction of 'picture element' [URL 4.1]) arranged in a rectangular array with a certain height and width (Figure 4.2). The raster file is simply a numerical array of data applying to each pixel, arranged in a particular order. Each pixel may be represented by one or more bits of information, representing the brightness of the image at that point and possibly including colour information encoded as RGB triples.

Figure 4.2 Image pixels

A digital colour image is composed of numeric data per pixel consisting of RGB colour values, usually three 8-bit numbers. An example is (255, 255, 0), meaning (Red = 255, Green = 255, Blue = 0) to denote one yellow pixel. A byte (8 bits) can contain numeric values from 0 to 255. A bit (short for binary digit) is the smallest unit of data in a computer. A bit has a single binary value, either 0 or 1 [URL 4.1]. The complete image file contains a specified RGB colour value for every pixel, or location, in the image grid, organised in rows and columns. File formats vary, but the header of the file contains information specifying the number of rows and columns (the image size, like 300 x 200) and how these are organised, and it is followed by huge strings of data representing the RGB values of every pixel. The viewing software then arranges

the RGB pixel values accordingly to create the image [URL 4.2]
An image in black and white uses only 1 bit per pixel, since there
is either image or no image (the switch is on or off). This type of
image is a so-called line tone image. For grey tone images more
information per pixel has to be stored. If one bit can give two values
(black and white) two bits will give 2 x 2 = 4 values, the black and
white and two intermediate tones. When using 3 bits per pixel we
are able to show 2 x 2 x 2 grey values, so 8 in total (Figure 4.3).
A common situation is 256 grey tones, which can be represented
by one byte (8 bits). For colour images, using RGB mode, we need
for each of the three colours 8 bits, bringing the total to 24 bits per
pixel, i.e. three bytes. This brings the total possible number of
colours to 256^3, that is 16,777,216. The number of bits used to
describe each pixel is referred to as the colour depth or bit depth
of the representation. In the references to bit depth found in, for
example, advertising literature, the confusing situation may arise
where bit depth may refer to each of RGB separately or else to
the combination. So '8-bit' could mean the same as '24-bit'.

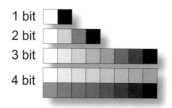

Figure 4.3 The concept of bit depth

   The quality of a raster image is based partly on the correct
colour description for each pixel, but also on the size of the pixels
used to describe the image. Generally it can be stated that the
more pixels used for the description of an image of a certain size,
the better the quality of the image representation (Figure 4.4). It
will be clear that a high-resolution image (many pixels used for
the description) consumes much memory. Resolution is mostly
described as dpi, standing for dots per inch. So theoretically,
a colour image of 1″ x 1″ with a resolution of 100 dpi and a
colour depth of 24 bits (= 3 bytes) consumes 100 x 100 x 3
= 30,000 bytes (= 30 kB). In reality the (uncompressed) file
will be somewhat bigger, since extra header information is added.

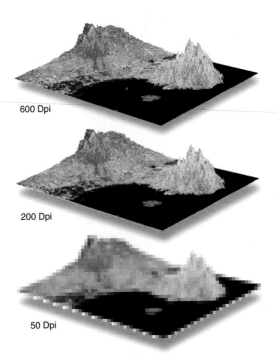

600 Dpi

200 Dpi

50 Dpi

Figure 4.4 Image resolution

Digital notation of colour

To get a clear idea about how colour is 'seen' by the scanner and the camera, a short explanation of the digital notation of colour is given here. In the following chapter (on output) similar notations are used.

A scanner and a digital camera work very much the same way as do our eyes. Behind the lens is an array of receptor units. A receptor is a body or surface sensitive to radiation. In biology a receptor is a specialised cell or group of cells that translates a certain type of stimulus received from the environment into nerve impulses [URL 4.3]. Each receptor unit in the scanner or camera is made of three smaller receptors which, like the cones in our eyes, are each stimulated by red, green, or blue light. The scanner or digital camera records the amount of light stimulation (i.e. the intensity) received by each receptor during the picture-taking process.

The recording process in a scanner or camera is based on digital numbers per pixel, as explained in the previous section.

Detectors				Detectors			
Colour	Red	Green	Blue	Colour	Red	Green	Blue
1. Black	0	0	0	5. Cyan	0	1	1
2. Red	1	0	0	6. Magenta	1	0	1
3. Green	0	1	0	7. Yellow	1	1	0
4. Blue	0	0	1	8. White	1	1	1

Table 4.1 3-bit colour

In a 3-bit system (one bit for each of R, G and B), the scanner or camera would record a 0 for light reflection below a pre-set intensity threshold and a 1 above it. The result would be a camera or scanner that could only record images with eight colours (Table 4.1).

If each receptor could encode using two bits, it could detect four levels of intensity per colour. The result would expand the number of detectable colours to 64, i.e. 4^3. In the part of the complete colour table reproduced here (Table 4.2), the colours described by name would give rise to the encoded result listed. This is called 6-bit colour. Warm Green would be described with the following 6 bits: '011100' (RGB: R = 01, G = 11, B = 00).

Detectors				Detectors			
Colour	R	G	B	Colour	R	G	B
1. Black	00	00	00	10. Warm Med. Gr.	01	10	00
2. Dark Red	01	00	00	11. Khaki Green	10	10	00
3. Medium Red	10	00	00	12. Orange	11	10	00
4. Red	11	00	00	13. Green	00	11	00
5. Dark Green	00	01	00	14. Warm Green	01	11	00
6. Olive	01	01	00	15. Yellow-Green	10	11	00
7. Brown	10	01	00	16. Yellow	11	11	00
8. Red Orange	11	01	00	17. Dark Blue	00	00	01
9. Medium Green	00	10	00	etc.			

Table 4.2 Encoding of colours in a 6-bit system

To allow a very wide range of colours, each digital camera or scanner detector encodes light intensity in a binary number consisting of one byte for each of R, G and B. Such a 24-bit device could then detect 16,777,216 different colours, at least in theory.

Here is one colour code to illustrate this:

Red 11110111   **Green 11100101**   **Blue 00000101**

So this yellow to the camera or scanner is:

111101111110010100000101

To make this more understandable we can convert to base-10 (our familiar decimal system) to yield the following:

Red 247   **Green 229**   **Blue 005**

Sometimes these intensity levels are expressed as percentages:

Red 96%   **Green 89%**   **Blue 2%**

In daily life the most used system is the decimal system that probably arose from counting on our fingers. Following the introduction of the concept of zero by Arab mathematicians this system now uses ten numerals and is termed base-10. The system used and described before in this chapter is the binary system, working with two numerals, 0 and 1 (base-2). Any base is actually possible, but one that is in common use in computing science is the base-16 system, i.e. the hexadecimal system. This requires 16 different numerals to represent it. Instead of inventing new symbols, the system uses the decimal numerals 0 to 9 then adds the letters A to F (Table 4.3). As in the decimal system the position of the numerals has significance. For example, decimal number 247 is made up of $(2 \times 10^2) + (4 \times 10) + 7$. Base-16 hexadecimal number E2B is made up of $(E \times 16^2) + (2 \times 16) + B$. In decimal notation this is $(14 \times 16^2) + (2 \times 16) + 11$, so 3627. The hexadecimal system has the advantage that all decimal numbers between 0 and 255 can be represented by a number consisting of no more than two digits. For an extensive explanation of the system see URL 4.4.

Decimal																						
0 1 2 3 4 5 6 7 8 9 10 11 12 13 14 15 16 17 18..26..28..31 32...

Hexadecimal																						
0 1 2 3 4 5 6 7 8 9 A B C D E F 10 11 12..1A .1C .1F 20...

Table 4.3 The decimal and hexadecimal systems

Here is our yellow in the hexadecimal notation:

Red F7   **Green E5**   **Blue 05**

The hexadecimal number F7, in decimal notation, is equivalent to (15 x 16) + 7, so 247. Similarly, E5 is equivalent to 229 and 05 is equivalent to 005.

Scanners and image resolution

Scanners are used to convert hardcopy images into digital form. The market offers a large variety of scanners, with differences in price, performance and quality. Considering the position of the original we can talk about flatbed scanners, drum scanners, sheet-feed scanners and hand-held scanners. There are scanners that work with reflected light for opaque images; others work with backlight for transparent originals. Some scanners offer both options. Flatbed scanners are the most common, and are designed to scan anything that will lie flat. Drum scanners are more accurate but much more expensive. They tend to be most used for very high quality production in the graphics industry, so they will not be treated further here.

Standard flatbed scanners work by reflection (Figure 4.5). The image you want to scan is laid face down on a glass plate and covered, so that no light can leak under the image and cause loss of contrast. An array of light sensitive electronic elements known as CCDs (Charge Coupled Devices) is fitted into a bar that lies

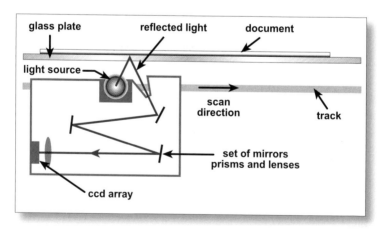

Figure 4.5 The principle of a flatbed scanner

under the glass plate and occupies the entire width of the scanning area. A CCD is a light sensitive silicon solid-state device composed of many small receptors that generate the scanned image pixels. Linked to this array is a narrow beam of bright light that illuminates the image from under the glass. The light that is reflected back from the image is measured by the CCD array. The light falling on a receptor is converted into a charge pulse which is then measured by the CCD electronics and represented by a value; the higher the value the more intense the light (Figure 4.6). The more light reflected back to the CCDs, the more electrical current they create. During scanning, the entire CCD array with its light source moves from top to bottom of the image. In this way, the scanner can measure the light intensities reflected from various parts of the image. The value of each receptor at each position of the array is translated into a grey value and stored as the specification for that specific pixel. All pixels are put together in columns and rows and the PC can now treat this collection like any other bitmap graphic.

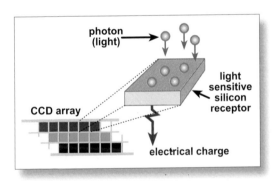

Figure 4.6 The principle of a CCD

When scanning for colour the reflected light has to be translated into R, G and B values. Different colours reflect different intensities of light in different wavelengths. The first generation of scanners had to make three passes to get the whole image, one for each colour. Coloured filters were used to expose for each of R, G and B. The newer generation scanners need only a single pass and they scan the different colour components at the same time. The first category of single-pass scanners split the reflected light into three beams that are each filtered and measured by a CCD. The separate colour values for each pixel are then combined to the RGB value for that specific pixel. Another type of single-pass scanners makes use of a linear CCD array with three embedded colour filters (a trilinear array) that captures image data one row of pixels at a time, one each for red, green, and blue (Figure 4.6).

A rather new development in sensor technology is the Contact Image Sensor (CIS) that began to be used in flatbed scanners in the late 1990s. A scanner fitted with a CIS does not use a fluorescent lamp to produce the white light but uses light-emitting diodes instead. The mirrors and lenses of a CCD scanner are replaced with an array of image sensors that lies just under the original to be scanned. The sensors catch the reflected light directly. The result is a light and thin scanner that is energy-efficient and cheap to manufacture. It is, however, not yet capable of emulating the performance of the better quality CCD scanners in resolution and colour depth [URL 4.5].

Most mid-price flatbed scanners have an optical resolution of 600 to 1200 dots per inch. This means that for every inch of the CCD array, the scanner takes 600 to 1200 light samples. The higher the number of dots per inch (higher scan resolution) the more detailed the digital image will be. Scanners offer the option to scan in a lower resolution than the maximum resolution of the scanner. The scanner continues to use all its CCDs but resamples to a lower resolution. A 600 dpi scanner has 600 dpi CCD cells, and when you scan at 120 dpi it must resample the 600 dpi scan line to 120 dpi.

Resampling is a drastic procedure that actually recalculates all of the image's pixel data values to produce a different size of image. For example, resampling may resize an image from 300 x 300 to 100 x 100. Or to put it another way, a block of 3 x 3 pixels (i.e. 9 pixels) reduces to a single pixel. Therefore the image reduces to one-third of its original size. If you want to keep the same image size, the pixels become three times larger (in x and y), so the apparent result is a loss of detail. One big advantage of resampling in this way is a big reduction in data volume: in our example, 90,000 pixels reduce to 10,000 pixels.

Resampling is just interpolation and in principle it can be applied to enlargement as well as to reduction. The only difference is that reducing image size discards data and detail (replaces many dots with a few, sometimes called downsampling), while increasing size to a larger image must fabricate additional data (replaces a few dots with many, sometimes called upsampling). The image is simply larger but no additional detail is possible without another scan, of course. Most scanners can use interpolation artificially to boost the resolution of the scanned image. The software looks at the colour samples and calculates colour differences between neighbouring samples. The extra dots increase the numerical resolution of the image but there is no real extra detail. Interpolated scans tend to have a blurred appearance when enlarged on the viewing screen.

When the scanned image has to be viewed on screen, and not used for printing, resampling is the only option because of the low resolution of the screen. For printing, there is a general rule concerning the minimum scan resolution of an image. Resampling is not necessarily bad, but it may not always be necessary. The standard rule when scanning for printing is that you must scan for the capability of the specific output device, using scanning resolution dpi = lpi (lines per inch) x 1.5. The extra 50% is to accommodate the printer driver's resampling when it creates the halftone screen image (Chapter 5). Some experts argue that a 2.5 to 4.0 factor is better (giving more sharpness in the fine details). One big problem with lpi is that you cannot find lpi mentioned in the printer specifications, because lpi is not dependent purely on the hardware. Instead lpi varies according to how the graphic software and printer driver choose to use the hardware. There is, however, much uniformity in commercial practice. Scanned images are typically sent to 1200 or 2400 dpi imagesetters for publication. The resolution has to be high in order to generate the individual dots of halftone screens (Chapter 5). A general standard, for example for printing magazines, is that there are 133 lines of these dots per inch. In this case, then, scanning at 133 x 1.5 = 200 dpi is theoretically correct. It does not make sense to scan at a much higher resolution (creating a large file) only to have to lose data again later. To be on the safe side, however, it is common practice to scan at somewhat higher resolutions than the theoretical minimum.

Scanners can be bought in different quality ranges and prices. The quality of a scanner is important when the images at a later stage are used for display in, for example, an electronic atlas or when they are printed. A very important element is of course the CCD array, in combination with the light source. The correctness of recording colour partly depends on the combination of these two. Also the way in which the CCD array and the light source are transported under the glass plate is of great importance. If this system is not stable there will be distortion in one direction, which is highly undesirable if planimetric accuracy is essential, as in the scanning of aerial photographs. With an unstable system, the distortion will differ every time, so no accurate geo-referencing can be performed. It will be obvious that the price of a scanner is generally determined by the quality of the components used in the scanner.

Digital cameras

A digital camera is a cross between a conventional camera and a scanner, combining image capture with digitising. Instead of using film, a digital camera stores images in digital form, either in its own internal memory or on a solid-state memory card. In a conventional camera light passes through a lens onto a light sensitive film that reacts differently according to the different wavelengths of the light that hits it. The light causes a chemical reaction to take place on the surface of the film, creating a so-called 'latent image'. Once the film has been developed, this film forms an image (either negative or positive, depending on the type of film used) that can be printed or projected.

A digital camera works in a similar way, but electronically. Light is focused through a lens onto a two-dimensional array of CCDs. A 640 x 480 array, for example, contains 307,200 CCDs. Each CCD in the array has in front a red, green or blue filter [URL 4.6] and reacts to the light within that specific wavelength range (Figure 4.7). The latest development is the use of CMY filters. These allow more light energy to pass so enable higher shutter speeds. For the final image the three colours are combined per pixel. Since only one colour per CCD can be recorded, the other two colours are extrapolated from the adjacent CCDs. The data from the CCDs are passed to the camera's logic circuitry, where the data are compressed. Most cameras use the JPEG (Joint Photographic Experts Group) compression format, which takes

COLOUR BASICS FOR GIS USERS

Figure 4.7 A CCD frame and an enlargement of part of the two-dimensional CCD array.

as much redundant data out of the image as possible to reduce the amount of storage space. The degree of compression depends on the quality of the final image you want. Most cameras use 8 to 1 or higher compression. Memory is more expensive than film, so the less memory the image takes up the better. The advantage of memory above film, however, is that memory can be used more often, film only once.

Once compressed, the image is stored as a series of digital binary codes in memory. This can be a camera's internal memory, a removable memory card, a Compact Flash Card, a mini-cd or even a conventional 3.5 inch floppy disk. Once the data are stored, they can be downloaded to a computer via a special cable. The data can now be decompressed and edited, inserted in a project or printed. Nowadays professional hand-held digital cameras can have resolutions up to 5.47 megapixel (5,470,000 pixels). Studio cameras, directly linked to a computer, have resolutions up to 8000 x 6000 pixels. Data coming from these types of cameras could use over 200 MB of memory for a single image. The hard disk of the computer is used as storage space. For outdoor work such a camera can be attached to a laptop computer.

Other methods of collecting raster and vector data

Scanners and digital cameras, also the scanners used in aircraft and satellites, collect raster data. Vector data can be derived from these, either automatically or with human interaction, e.g. screen digitising. Vector data input for use in a GIS can also be collected by manual digitising using a digitising tablet. Increasingly, vector data are collected directly in the field using the latest surveying technology, including GPS-based systems. In addition, it often happens that existing data are used, perhaps made available on video, CD-ROM or taken from the World Wide Web. These data will be in either raster or vector format.

Raster editing and image processing

It is normal practice to manipulate the raster data resulting from a digital camera or scanner before outputting an image. The editing or processing stage may be carried out using purely graphic image processing software such as Adobe Photoshop. In the GIS context, the raster images may result from a digital photograph, from scanning a photograph, map or other paper image, or from the manipulation of satellite scanner or radar data. Some of the many algorithms used in image processing are thinning (or skeletonisation), edge detection and contrast enhancement. These are usually implemented in software but may also use special purpose hardware for speed. Image processing techniques as such are beyond the scope of this book. Interested readers are referred to the many specialised texts on the subject, such as Sangwine and Horne (1998). Even although the basic operations are often rather simple, because of the large amount of data in a typical raster dataset, especially for RGB data, the computer has much work to do. Once new values of RGB are calculated, they can be output on the screen and, if required, converted into CMYK and printed. Figure 4.8 illustrates some typical image enhancement procedures for satellite data, using the RGB/IHS environment in Erdas Imagine software and, as original data, a Landsat MSS dataset from the Erdas samples.

The illustrations are as follows:

a. The original three-band composite image
b. Intensity stretch applied to the original
c. Saturation stretch applied to the original
d. The original stretched in each of RGB
e. The image of c stretched in each of RGB

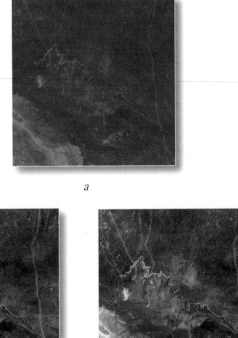

a

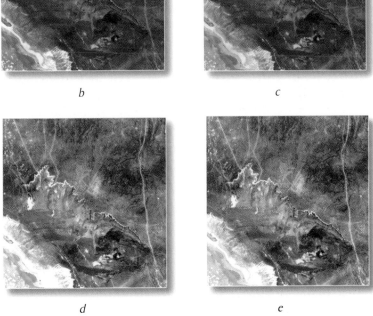

b   *c*

d   *e*

Figure 4.8 Four enhancements of an original Landsat MSS colour composite

RGB or CMY?

A digital camera or colour scanner records in RGB. The resulting image can be displayed directly on a display screen (Chapter 2), with or without some image editing or processing. For printing on paper, however, we must use CMY(K). If you know that the image will be printed, the question is whether or not to record directly in CMY, provided the software allows this. All the image corrections could then be done in CMY, which gives better control over the result. However, you should bear in mind that, if working with CMY images in image editing software, the image constantly is converted to RGB to make it possible to view it on the monitor. Apart from this you may not want hardcopy output, or you might want to use the image for an Internet Web page, that uses RGB.

In the first place you must realise that whatever the software does to the data, the receptors usually originally recorded in RGB. When converting RGB to CMY, a simple calculation can be performed using the concept of the colour cube, as explained in Chapter 3. The RGB colours are first converted to CMY values by subtracting RGB respectively from the maximum value 255. So the value for Cyan = 255 − value for Red, the value for Magenta = 255 − value for Green and finally the value for Yellow = 255 − value for Blue.

Let us take the yellow colour used previously as an example:
Red 247   **Green 229**   **Blue 005**

Converted to CMY this gives:
Cyan 008   **Magenta 026**   **Yellow 250**

As already shown in Chapter 3, however, this easy calculation does not give good results in practice. A first improvement can be achieved using the concept of Under Colour Removal (UCR), by which black ink (K) is used as much as possible to replace the grey component of the printing ink combinations. In its very simplest application, using the given yellow as an example, the highest denominator 'grey', consisting of equal amounts of CMY, is replaced by black. In the example, this grey consists of 008C + 008M + 008Y.

The yellow would now be printed as follows:
Cyan 000   **Magenta 018**   **Yellow 242**   **Black 008**

In practice, the result usually needs some adjustment to take account of the characteristics of the particular printing method being used.

A more complex procedure is called Grey Component Replacement (GCR). GCR is a widely used procedure in the colour separation process in the commercial graphics industry. The process uses the black to replace cyan, magenta and yellow not only where they all overlap (as done in UCR), but also to replace the grey component everywhere in the image. The process uses parameters based on the characteristics of the printing inks used. The application of GCR improves image quality and reduces the amount of CMY inks used. It helps to produce more stable neutral colours and minimises colour shifts due to slight ink variability while printing.

A fundamental problem is that even using UCR or GCR the colours on the CMYK output are not the same as on the RGB monitor (see also Chapter 2). This results in different colour gamuts on paper and on screen (Chapter 3). More advanced colour conversion software takes this into account, so reduces the monitor colour gamut as an intermediate step in order to make all colours printable in CMYK. However, a corresponding extension of the gamut might not happen when you convert from CMYK to RGB, with the result that the screen colours will not occupy the full possible colour space. In other words, the data lost in the conversion from RGB to CMYK cannot be retrieved when you convert back.

The preferred solution is to do all digital image corrections, retouching, and manipulations in RGB and then output the files to RGB or CMYK using the appropriate output device. Values of RGB and CMYK on any image can be displayed on viewing software such as freeware 'ShowImage' from efg [URL 4.7].

Chapter 5

Colour output

In a GIS, the interface with the user is the display screen. At present, Cathode Ray Tube (CRT) technology is still dominant, although liquid crystal diode (LCD) displays are becoming common (e.g. on laptop computers). Hardcopy paper output of the result of an analysis, often a map, can be produced on a variety of different printers. If many copies are required, offset printing must be used. Especially if the printing company is far away, or if you want to send the result over the Internet, then the map has to be output to a digital file in the desired format. This chapter treats all of these possible outputs.

Displays

The interface between the computer and the user is the graphic display device. Without this device it would be like working with a black box, and many interactions with the spatial data would be impossible. To gain a better understanding of how colour is generated on these devices and why we see the colours on them as they appear, the different technologies are treated in detail here. It is important to note that different devices may produce different colours from the same data.

Graphics card or board

When working in an application on your PC the result is directly visualised on the monitor and the route from application to monitor seems short. In reality quite some calculating and steps are required: the way is long and indirect [URL 5.1]. The information from the application is sent through the graphics driver that converts the digital data into a format understandable to the graphics board, where the data are temporarily stored. The

Graphics Processing Unit (GPU) translates the data into pixels. For a monitor with a resolution of 1152 x 864 a total number of 995,328 pixels are generated. These pixel data are finally sent to the monitor where the image is created, in fact refreshed many times per second. The higher the refresh rate, expressed in hertz (frequency per second), the more stable, i.e. free of flicker, the image appears.

Most CRT monitors create images from an analogue signal, so the pixels calculated in the GPU have to be converted from a digital to an analogue signal. This conversion is done by the Random Access Memory Digital-to-Analogue Converter (RAMDAC). This microchip combines a Static RAM (SRAM) that contains a colour table and three Digital-to-Analogue Converters (the DAC) for Red, Green and Blue. The analogue data are sent to the three electron guns that produce the image. When the display is True Color (i.e. 24-bit), the colour table and therefore the SRAM is not needed, so the data go directly to the DAC. For displays such as LCD that can handle digital data, the digital-to-analogue conversion is in principle redundant and another type of graphics board is needed (Figure 5.1).

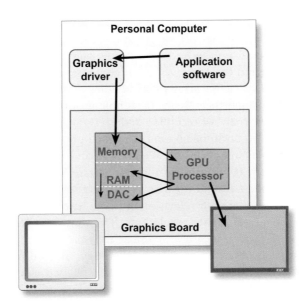

Figure 5.1 The principle of a graphics board

If you are using a 75 Hz, 17-inch monitor at 1152 x 864 resolution, the number of bits that have to be processed by the graphics board is enormous. For 24-bit colour the full screen requires 23,887,872 bits, and this 75 times per second!

CRT display

Coloured raster refresh cathode ray tube display screens are used to produce multicoloured non-permanent 'softcopy' output that may, for example, be computer-generated maps or remotely sensed images. These devices are often called colour monitors. They are also used in video games and computer graphics in general, and their cost is quite low considering the advanced technology involved, which of course is basically the same as television technology. There are, however, signs that production of this type of monitor will stop and the LCD and other flat panel displays will take over the leading role [URL 5.2].

The general principle of a refresh CRT is that a scanning electron beam of varying density of electrons (to produce variations in intensity) strikes a phosphorescent material on a screen. To produce multicoloured images, three electron guns are needed, one each for red, green and blue, and the screen is covered with a closely packed regular array of phosphor dots, each of which glows either red or green or blue. To ensure that the electron beam from the 'red' gun strikes only those dots which glow red, and the same for green and blue, a metal shadow mask, drilled with a dense array of small holes, is positioned between the guns and the screen. Each hole in the shadow mask corresponds to a 'triad' of red, blue and green dots. The angle of incidence of the electron beam controls which phosphor dot is caused to glow behind each hole (Figure 5.2 and URL 5.3). This type of technology is often called the Flat Square Tube (FST). FST monitors have been around for many years and rely on technology similar to that used in your television at home, except that they can display images at higher resolutions. The view on a FST monitor can, however, look a little fuzzy, especially when dealing with small details. A variation of the technology, as used in the Sony Trinitron CRT, is to use horizontally aligned electron beams and an aperture grille with vertical slots instead of the conventional shadow mask. These monitors produce a less fuzzy, much sharper image.

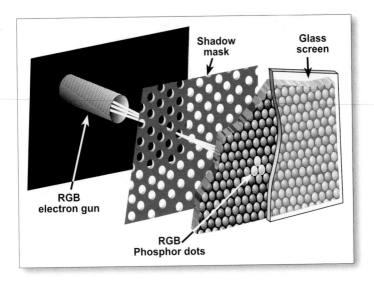

Figure 5.2 The principle of a refresh CRT

The phosphor dots in a FST monitor screen are very small and spaced very close together, commonly of the order of 0.28 mm for the spacing between dots of the same colour (Figure 5.3). This spacing is known as the pitch of the screen (or dot pitch) and it determines the sharpness of the details that can be shown. Each dot glows independently, and the light from all three colours combines additively to produce the colours we perceive on the screen.

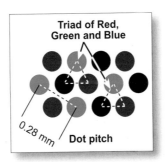

Figure 5.3 Dot pitch

If each electron gun is controlled by one memory plane (the so-called three-bit system), each gun can be either off or on when it is directed at any particular hole of the shadow mask. Therefore each associated phosphor dot either glows or does not glow. The result of this is eight possible colours, as shown in Table 5.1 (the output equivalent of Table 4.1).

Activated gun			Perceived	Activated gun			Perceived
Red	Green	Blue	Colour	Red	Green	Blue	Colour
0	0	0	Black	0	1	1	Cyan
1	0	0	Red	1	0	1	Magenta
0	1	0	Green	1	1	0	Yellow
0	0	1	Blue	1	1	1	White

Table 5.1 Colours of a three-bit-system

If there are two memory planes per gun, that is a so-called bit depth of two bits per gun for every phosphor dot position, there are four possible binary numbers per gun (00, 01, 10, 11). 00 is used for 'off', 11 is used for 'fully on'. 01 and 10 are used for two intermediate power levels, to activate intermediate electron densities, therefore causing intermediate light intensities from the phosphor dots. With these four possible states per gun, there are 4^3, i.e. 64, possible colours.

A common arrangement is the 24-bit display, which has 8 bits per colour, allowing a palette of 16,777,216 colours. In many systems you will find the possibility to choose a 32-bit 'True Color' display. This is exactly the same as 24-bit colour for use on a display screen. The extra byte, called the alpha channel, is used for control and special effects information. Not all of the 16.8 million 24-bit colours may be displayable at one time. The reason for this is that the electronics of the system may not be able to cope with so many intensity levels, which require a powerful processor. Simple graphics boards have one byte (8 bits) for colour control. This allows only 256 simultaneously displayable colours. Even if your system allows the display of more colours, it is still possible to limit your selection to 256 (or fewer) colours. In this case the system will automatically select the 256 colours to be used. In many cases, these colours are sufficient. Processing will be faster, and the system may allow a higher display resolution with 256 colours than with 16.8 million.

A variation of this technique is one that allows the user to select which 256 colours to use from the complete palette. This creates a 'lookup table' (LUT) that connects each of the 256 colour codes to a particular output colour. Much graphics software was first developed when this was a limitation, so it is still common to find the LUT system in use. It is also possible to create a LUT using two bytes, therefore allowing 65,536 colours. Even although nowadays most PCs have the necessary software, graphics board and screen to support displaying all 16.8 million colours at once, many users prefer to use LUTs because of the faster processing. To use this system to its full advantage, you have to be able to select from a large colour palette. If you have a small basic palette of 256 colours and you want to create a colour which lies somewhere between the given colours, the system will approximate the colour you want by 'dithering', i.e. by creating a regular pattern of pixels of the nearest colours so that the final result will be what you want, though rather 'grainy' in appearance (Figure 5.4). Since the basic dither pattern occupies several pixels the result looks unsharp for very fine lines and small symbols and text.

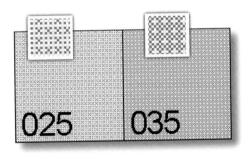

Figure 5.4 Dither patterns based on part of Figure 7.3

The apparent sharpness of a colour display is influenced by a complex set of factors, including resolution, dot pitch and convergence. As described in Chapter 4, the pixel is the smallest possible addressable unit on the screen. The more pixels used when creating an image, the sharper the image. The size of the pixels is usually expressed in pixels per inch (72 pixels/inch is a widely accepted standard). This is sometimes referred to as pixel resolution, but since the term resolution is also used to express the number of columns and rows of pixels in a display, confusion can arise. As regards dot pitch, a screen with a 0.26 mm dot pitch will give a much sharper image than a screen with a 0.38 mm dot pitch, but it will cost much more. Convergence relates to how closely the three electron beams focus on the individual holes of the metal mask. Poor convergence results in fuzzy images or a three-colour blur, especially near the edges of the screen.

The general quality of an image on a monitor depends also on a number of other factors, including:

- the actual hues of the phosphor dots;
- the maximum usable brightness while maintaining good sharpness;
- contrast, i.e. the luminance ratio between a fully illuminated dot and the black screen;
- grey linearity (how well it displays proportional levels of brightness);
- tracking (balanced intensity of all three electron guns);
- the quickness of reaction of the phosphor dots to variations in density of the electrons, coupled with absence of too long 'post glowing' when the electron beam is switched off;
- the incorporation of glare protection screen coatings or anti-reflective panels, to reduce the influence of background room lighting, the so-called ambient light (which increases luminance and decreases contrast);
- the quality of the white screen colour (how close it is to white paper);
- whether there is a noticeable flicker (a function of the refresh rate);
- what controls are available for colour, contrast and sharpness;
- the refresh rate, which should be at least 64 Hz for a 14 or 15 inch monitor and 75 Hz for a 17 inch monitor;
- the type of technology used, FST or Trinitron;
- the working environment, i.e. the light conditions in the room.

GIS users and cartographers are very demanding customers when it comes to screen displays. As well as good colour, high resolution and sharpness, they also prefer large screens, 17-inch or more if possible. This is the length of the screen diagonal, so a 17-inch screen will have dimensions of approximately 14 x 11 inches. A good standard resolution for a 17-inch display is 1024 pixels horizontally and 768 vertically (usually written simply as 1024 x 768). This converts to approximately 72 pixels/inch both horizontally and vertically. The more powerful processing chips used on modern PCs allow even higher resolutions, for example 1152 x 864 or 1280 x 960. Smaller monitors achieve a comparable pixel size at a lower resolution, e.g. 800 x 600 on a 14-inch monitor. Therefore a small screen is less demanding of computer processing power than a large screen.

There is a relationship between dot pitch and resolution: a screen cannot display properly an image that has a higher (finer) resolution than the dot pitch. The maximum resolution setting on a monitor gives rise to a pixel size that corresponds to the dot pitch. A dot pitch of 0.28 mm is equivalent to 90 dots/inch, easily able to accommodate a screen resolution of 72 pixels/inch. A dot pitch of 0.38 mm, on the other hand, corresponds to only 67 dots/inch. In the case of a 15-inch screen with a dot pitch of 0.38 mm, the maximum resolution is therefore 800 x 600.

Flat Panel Displays

CRT displays use the basic technology of colour television. This is now approaching its limits. Larger screens than about 21 inch are not possible because the electron gun cannot scan fast enough to maintain a high refresh rate. With a lower refresh rate the image flickers. The dot pitch cannot be made any finer than it is already. A monitor that is near the present limits of size and dot pitch is very expensive. Furthermore, CRT monitors are heavy, bulky, produce heat and use a lot of electricity. Some industrial analysts see an analogy with steam railway locomotives. These developed over many years to a high state of perfection, but were replaced by new technology in the shape of diesel and electric locomotives. CRT displays will be replaced in the near future by the so-called Flat Panel Displays (FPDs) [URL 5.4]. LCD (Liquid Crystal Display) is already a familiar technology but there are many more ongoing developments, such as PDP (Plasma Display Panel), LED (Light Emitting Diode), EL (Electroluminescent Panel), VFD (Vacuum Fluorescent Display), DMD (Digital Micromirror Device) and FED (Field Emission Display) [URL 5.5]. These display panels are all rigid. Flexible displays, such as 'digital paper', are also being developed. Technology is progressing rapidly and there is no certainty that any of the present systems will achieve the final breakthrough. The outcome may well depend on which of the present (or new) technologies is adopted for domestic televisions. The growing electronic book market will also probably have an influence. In the rest of this section, the basic characteristics are summarised of the most important types of FPDs in production or under development at the time of writing.

Liquid Crystal Display panels

A very important impetus in the development of flat panel displays is the laptop computer market. The display of a laptop has to be lightweight, thin and flat, use little power and need no cooling fan. Liquid Crystal Displays (LCDs) were already in use for digital watches and pocket calculators. These depend on reflected light, and as a result the early colour displays based on this technology had very weak colour, and were only visible from directly in front. The breakthrough came with the development of active-matrix technology.

This technology is also known as Thin Film Transistor (TFT). The liquid crystals control the amount of polarised light that passes [URL 5.5]. A simplified explanation is to think of the naturally loosely ordered liquid crystals being forced to lie in

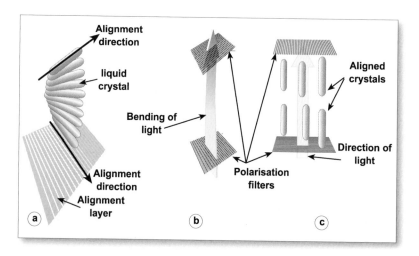

Figure 5.5 Liquid crystals

one direction along the molecular grooves of an alignment layer. When using a 'sandwich' with two alignment layers positioned perpendicular to each other, the crystals in between form a twist (Figure 5.5a). Polarised light that passes through the 'sandwich' is twisted too (Figure 5.5b). Therefore if polarisation filters are added on each side of the 'sandwich', parallel to the alignment layers, light passes through unimpeded. When voltage is applied to the 'sandwich' the crystals rearrange themselves (Figure 5.5c) and light passes without bending. The incoming polarised light is therefore blocked by the second filter. The degree of crystal rearrangement is controlled by the voltage applied.

A Liquid Crystal Display makes use of this technology. Light is sent through a layered structure from the back (Figure 5.6). Transparent electrodes on both sides of the liquid crystal 'sandwich' regulate the voltage at fixed x-y positions. Light that comes through the 'sandwich' passes through an array of red,

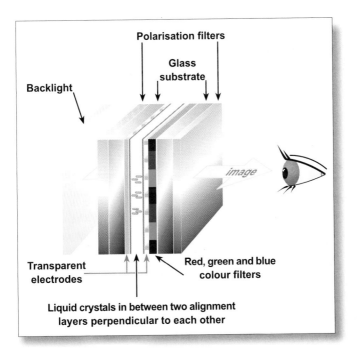

Figure 5.6 The principle of a Liquid Crystal Display

green and blue filters. The intensity of the light at each position determines the brightness. The image is therefore built up of RGB elements, like a CRT display. The result has good colour and high contrast, and can be viewed from the side (very important if more than one person at a time is viewing an image). These displays are not easy to manufacture. Any malfunction leads to a 'dead spot' on the screen. Now, however, the main manufacturers are improving the quality and bringing prices down. At the high end of the market, it is possible to buy a 21-inch LCD panel with high resolution (2048 x 1536), a refresh rate of 85 Hz and an ability to support simultaneous display of 16.8 million colours. More affordable is a 15-inch display with 1024 x 768 pixel resolution and 75 Hz refresh rate. These displays can definitely be used instead of CRT monitors. One advantage not so far mentioned of LCDs and of other flat panel displays over CRTs is that the fixed position of the pixels in relation to the RGB triads keeps the image sharp. In a CRT the pixel position depends on each scan of the electron beam being exactly the same as the previous one, which is difficult to achieve in practice, therefore the image can appear slightly fuzzy.

LCD technology does, however, have its limitations, apart from the manufacturing problems. The cost increases sharply with size, though this is not serious for laptop displays, which anyway are rather small. On lower cost displays, the screen image is not visible when viewed from the side at an angle of less than about $30°$, measured from the screen plane. This gives a total viewing angle of $120°$. A CRT monitor has in theory a viewing angle approaching $180°$ but in practice, because of reflection from the glass, $160°$ is normally taken to be the limit. This viewing angle is also achieved by the more expensive LCD displays. In a CRT display the phosphor dots continue glowing after the electron beam leaves them, but in a LCD each RGB element reacts immediately to voltage changes. Therefore rather high refresh rates (ideally at least 85 Hz) are needed for a perfectly stable image.

Gas plasma panels

Gas plasma panels (Figure 5.7) are now becoming affordable. They have a major advantage over LCDs in that they are fairly simple to make and manufacturing costs increase only linearly with size, so they are suitable for large displays, e.g. 42-inch diagonal. The simplest way to understand the principle of the Plasma Display Panel (PDP) is to think of it as a fluorescent lamp in the form of a 'sandwich'. Between the two glass plates there is a space of 0.1 mm containing a gas (argon or neon), where an electric discharge generates ultraviolet rays. The space is divided up into tiny elements, and on the rear glass plate there is a phosphor dot (red, green or blue) corresponding to each element. Power is supplied by two sets of parallel wires, one set horizontal, the other vertical. The gas – the plasma – is charged and, when a high enough voltage is put across it using the two wires, produces in each element a UV light 'flash'. The UV rays in turn activate the RGB phosphors to create visible light. The higher the voltage to each element, the more UV light is produced and the brighter the glow. Colour images are thus produced on the flat TV front screen. The viewing angle is better than 160°, it is bright and it can display any number of colours [URL 5.6].

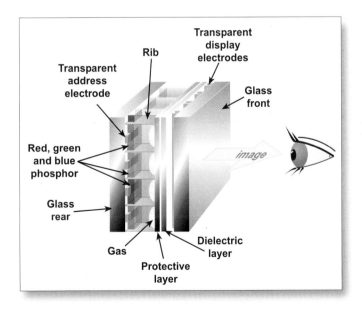

Figure 5.7 The gas plasma panel

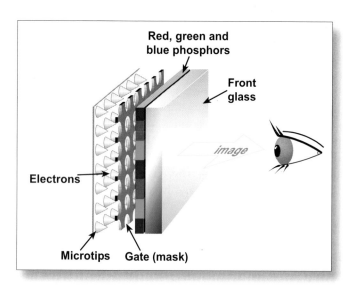

Figure 5.8 The principle of the Field Emission Display panel

Field Emission Display panel

Another type of flat panel is the Field Emission Display (FED). This uses cathode ray technology like a CRT, but instead of having a hot cathode emitting a single stream of electrons that are then swept across a screen, each phosphor dot has its own, individual, cold cathode (Figure 5.8 and URL 5.7). Colour is displayed by 'field sequential colour'. The display shows all the green information first, then redraws the screen with red followed by blue. An array of millions of cathodes is easier to make than an active-matrix LCD. It also uses aspects of existing technology, like the phosphor dots. The advantage is the low power consumption, large viewing angle (160°) and very bright display. The technology has much potential and research groups all over the world are working on its development, but at the time of writing only very small displays could be manufactured.

Other types of rigid displays

There is much research and experimentation going on in the field of flat, rigid display panels for special purposes. Some of the developments that have reached the production stage are mentioned here.

Digital Micromirror Device

This system produces a projected image on a screen and can be used, for example, for a so-called 'home cinema'. A DMD has a structure in which a chip is covered with tiny aluminium mirrors measuring 16 μm square, the number of these mirrors depending on the size of the chip. Each mirror can tilt independently between +10 degrees ('on') and −10 degrees ('off'). The digital signal tilts the mirrors between the 'on' and 'off' positions. When light from a projector hits a mirror in the 'on' stage, the light is reflected through a projection lens on to a screen, while in the 'off' stage the light is deflected to an area where it is fully absorbed. The amount of light reflected depends on the position of the mirror between 'on' and 'off'. The projected light is red, green and blue in quick succession, so creating the coloured image. The projected image can be quite large, typically 100-inch diagonal [URL 5.8].

Light Emitting Diode

Since Light Emitting Diode displays produce a very bright image they are already popular for outdoor use, e.g. in stadiums. A LED is a device that emits visible light when an electric current passes through it. The light is monochromatic, and for the displays three LEDs (red, green and blue) are combined in a so-called LED-dot. Most of the systems can handle at least 256 colours. The original LED technology is based on crystals but a new type, the OLED, is based on organic materials. OLED displays have several advantages apart from their brightness and wide viewing angle: they need little power, they can be made very thin and low-cost bulk manufacturing should be possible. It is expected that this technology will be suitable for all sizes of displays and it may replace LCD technology in the future [URL 5.9].

Flat flexible displays

"My own ideal would be a very thin, flexible, solid-state display which could be unrolled out of a sturdy cylindrical casing of a conveniently portable size, perhaps 40 cm long. This could be used at work or in the home, attached to a computer, for all the interactive and map design operations.... For field or car use you would be able to preload map data or other images you need on to a very compact, erasable, solid-state storage medium, requiring only a tiny computer..." (Brown, 1993). This wish is now becoming closer to reality. Research is being conducted into some display technologies that can be used on non-flat surfaces and even on flexible materials like paper. Two of the technologies that are furthest advanced in the field of 'digital paper' are mentioned here.

E ink

E ink makes use of the principle of a tiny hollow capsule filled with liquid. In the case of black and white displays, black and white pigment chips float in a clear liquid. The white chips carry a positive charge, the black chips a negative charge. The capsules are embedded in a substrate between electrodes. When opposite voltages are applied to the top and bottom electrodes the chips are attracted to opposite sides of the capsules, so giving rise to a black or white appearance (Figure 5.9). As the voltage difference becomes less, so the pigment chips float more freely and the resulting colour tends towards grey.

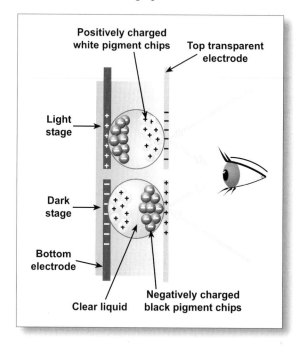

Figure 5.9 The principle of E ink, making use of two pigments

At the present stage of development, 256 grey values are possible. In the coloured version, the liquid in the capsules is coloured cyan, magenta or yellow and there are only white pigment chips (Figure 5.10). In use, the microcapsules are suspended in a liquid carrier medium with many of the properties of traditional ink so that it will adhere to any surface where regular ink can be screen-printed, then harden [URL 5.10]. A laminate has to be constructed, with raster electrode layers under and above the E ink layer. Power consumption is low since the display is entirely reflective and once an image is written no more power is required until the image is changed. E ink is already used for large commercial displays. As yet the resolution is not very high. Once displays with resolutions between 200 and 300 dpi can be made, especially in colour, then the technology will become suitable for electronic books and maps. The problem with colour displays is that the C, M and Y microcapsules have to be printed in a very fine, regular array. The image cannot yet change quickly so it is not suitable for video or animated displays, besides which a rapidly changing image requires more power.

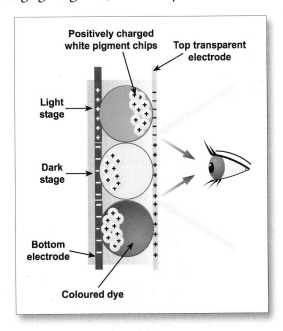

Figure 5.10 The principle of E ink, using coloured liquid

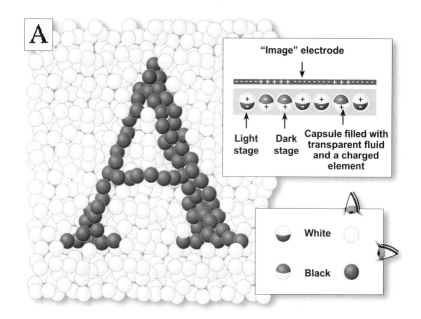

Figure 5.11 Electronic reusable paper

Gyricon

The Xerox Palo Alto Research Center (PARC) is working on a material called 'Gyricon', which they refer to as 'electronic reusable paper' (Figure 5.11 and URL 5.11). A Gyricon sheet is a thin layer of transparent plastic in which millions of small capsules are randomly scattered. In each of these oil-filled capsules a round bichromal bead can rotate. The beads have one half white, the other half black or else have two other contrasting colours. The two sides of a bead have opposite charges. When voltage is applied to the surface of the sheet in one of several ways, the bichromal beads rotate. For example, a charged 'pencil' can be moved over the surface causing one coloured side of the beads to rotate upward and therefore create writing, or else a charged 'wand' can move across the sheet to create an image. Images and text can also be formed by a process similar to laser printing. For a dynamic display a very fine grid of wires at the back of the sheet applies the charge. However it is created, the image remains until it is erased by a uniform charge or until a new image is made. This system is very suitable for electronic books, like the E ink described in the previous section. Like it, it is purely reflective and requires low power consumption. Also similar to the E ink system, coloured displays require a regular high-resolution array of cyan, magenta and yellow beads. More research and development are necessary before this can be achieved.

Colour printers

This chapter has dealt so far with so-called 'softcopies', temporary images not meant for eternal life. For a 'hardcopy' a permanent image has to be transferred to paper or another medium. If only a few paper copies of a small map or other graphic output from a GIS are required, you will make them on a colour printer. There is a very large general market for small format printers (A4 and A3) so prices have dropped considerably in recent years. However, the very large format printers that cartographers often require remain rather expensive items, although here also prices are dropping. In this section the main types of printer are described. Technical aspects are essential to understanding the problems and complexities of reproducing an image on the printed page, as is an understanding of additive RGB and subtractive CMY(K). The basic principles of the use of RGB and CMY plus the reason for the addition of black (K) ink in colour printers are all described in Chapter 2. The concepts of Under Colour Removal and Grey Component Replacement, as may be used in printer technology, are introduced in Chapter 4.

Dithering

The concept of dithering has already been discussed in the context of display screens (Figure 5.4). A similar process is necessary in many types of printers. The commonest printing principle is to print small C, M, Y and K dots. When overprinted, CMY dots produce R, G or B. Other colours are produced by printing CMYK dots in so-called dither patterns. From a distance the eye sees the sum of all the colours used, and the appearance is reasonably smooth, but on close viewing the patterns are clearly visible. A result of using dither patterns is that the resolution becomes less, because the basic pattern unit requires several dots. This further implies that small text and fine lines can be printed successfully in one of only six colours: C, M, R, G, B, K (Y is too light against a white background).

One major practical problem with dither patterns is that they are not the same on different printers. This, together with the fact that different printers use different CMY pigments, explains why the same image printed on two printers may not appear the same. Another problem with dither patterns is that they do not produce good results for light colours. A pale blue, for example, is produced by printing very widely spaced dots of C and M. To overcome this problem, some printers have extra printing heads containing very light C and M inks. These improve the printing quality (the claim is 'photographic quality' or 'photo-realistic') but they add to the price and to the running costs.

PostScript

Before starting to describe printers, it is important to establish that there are basically two types. The cheapest colour printers are the so-called Bitmap printers that print the same image as you see on your monitor but in the resolution of the printer. The quality of these printers is good but perhaps not good enough for very detailed maps. Curved or angled lines can appear 'ragged' or stepped. The high resolution of the new generation of Bitmap printers, from 400 dpi for colour and 600 dpi for black, overcomes this disadvantage, however. More important is that these printer types are not capable of printing PostScript data. If a PostScript file is sent directly to a Bitmap printer a very low-resolution image (mostly monitor resolution, 72 dpi), or in the worst cases a diagonal cross or a full colour rectangle, will be printed. Special effects such as gradient fills and semi-transparent overlay images may be printed very poorly, if at all.

Adobe PostScript is a widely used output file format in the graphics industry. The main characteristics of PostScript are mentioned here but for a more complete description see the Glossary and URL 5.12. PostScript (PS) or Encapsulated PostScript (EPS) is a so-called Page Description Language (PDL), a higher programming language that enables the graphic output of complete documents on a raster output device. PostScript describes documents not as pixels but as object-oriented data in ASCII format. The same PS file can be sent to many different types of output device. As part of the process, PS interpreter software converts the data into a form that the output device can deal with. A Raster Image Processor (RIP), usually incorporated in the output device itself, then converts the data into a raster image at the highest quality that the device is capable of producing. In the case of a colour printer, each printing dot is individually controlled.

PostScript, being hardware independent, can be used on any output device that is equipped with a RIP. That is why PS files can be printed on a low resolution (150 dpi) as well as on a high resolution (2400 dpi) output device. Not only is PostScript hardware independent but it is also scale independent. This means that, even with extreme enlargement, the quality of the output will be high, without ragged lines or blurry fills. When using PostScript it is worth bearing in mind that, once a PS file is made, in most cases the software that made it can no longer access it. The only way to change something is by changing the ASCII source code or by making changes in the native (original) file and then making a new PS file.

Inkjet printers

These are the most common printers in use at the time of writing. Techniques used in these types of printers differ, as well as the quality obtained. The technology is developing rapidly, so it is advisable to read the technical journals to keep track of the latest advances. Inkjet Bitmap printers are cheap to buy, at least in small formats. The PS printers are more expensive but for all printers the price/quality ratio continues to improve.

Drop-on-demand

The cheapest printers are the two types of drop-on-demand printers. In both cases they squirt tiny drops of ink on to the paper. In one type, often called bubble-jet (Figure 5.12), a heating element turns the ink into gas in a chamber and the resulting pressure forces a tiny drop of ink through a nozzle on to the paper [URL 5.13].

In the other type, the necessary pressure is applied by a very small piezo-electric diaphragm. In both cases, the print head tracks across the paper leaving dots where required. There are usually four printing heads, one each for C, M, Y and K (black).

Black is added as a fourth ink because as we have noted earlier, CMY together produce a very dark brown instead of a good black. It is also more economical to use only one colour to make black rather than to use all of the CMY inks. The ink drops are of equal

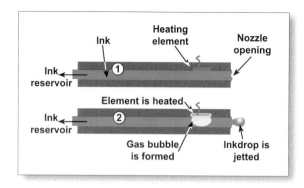

Figure 5.12 How inkjet works

Figure 5.13 Examples of printing head nozzle configurations

size and where more ink is required more drops are squirted on the paper. The individual drops are very small, so in any printed area what the eye sees is a kind of average result of all the inks used, including unprinted white paper.

Printer resolution is expressed in dots per inch (dpi). 600 dpi is typical, though the black ink may print at 1200 dpi (or even higher), therefore producing very sharp black lines and text. Figure 5.13 shows several printer nozzle configurations. The resolution is the closest distance between nozzles. Printing technology is always developing and Canon, for example, has introduced the 'Drop Modulation' technique based on thermal technology.

The printing head has two (instead of one) heating elements, and can produce drops of different sizes (Figure 5.14). Small dots are used in areas where very little ink is required, large dots are used to produce darker, more saturated colours. This technology is specially used for photo-realistic printing.

Because these printers use liquid ink, the ink droplets tend to splash, spread and sink in on hitting the paper. The general effect

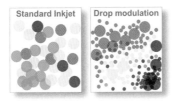

Figure 5.14 Difference between standard inkjet and drop modulation

is to make the colours darker and duller and the printed image as a whole less sharp than you would like. The effects are less and a better image is therefore produced if specially coated paper is used. On this type of paper the ink remains on the surface and gives more vivid colours and a sharper image (Figure 5.15). The quality of the inkjet printers has developed to such a high standard that, provided special paper is used, they easily can compete with the dye-sublimation printers when it comes to printing photo-realistic images.

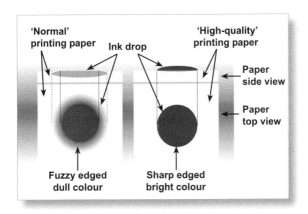

Figure 5.15 Difference between 'Normal' and 'High-quality' printing paper

Continuous flow

A second main type of inkjet printer produces a continuous flow of ink that is pressed through a small nozzle. The nozzle tracks very rapidly back and forward across the paper. A jet of up to 120,000 homogeneous drops per second develops. The drops pass through a constant electrical field with a very high voltage, bending the drops into a container for reuse. Whenever an image is needed on the paper the electrical field changes and the ink drops are no longer diverted but hit the paper. Since the ink flow is constant, not produced at intervals as in the drop-on-demand printers, this type of printer gives very good colour, very smooth flat tints and therefore photo-realistic quality. Even under magnification, you cannot see the individual dots on the paper: the cyan, magenta and yellow inks appear to be mixed. This type of printer is often used for the production of digital proofs, employed in the graphics industry to be shown to customers. A disadvantage is the minimum line thickness that can be produced, namely 0.1 mm. This might seem to be very fine, but when printing very small text, this will give problems. These printers are very expensive, due to the advanced technology used.

Phase change

A third type of inkjet printer is the phase change inkjet. In this case the ink is supplied as pigmented solid wax sticks. Heating melts the wax stick and drops of liquid wax are propelled on to the paper as with the piezo-electric type. As soon as the wax reaches the paper it cools and immediately hardens. This process produces output similar to the drop-on-demand technology, but a little coarser. The colours are very brilliant, since the ink is not partially absorbed by the printing medium, but remains on top as a thick layer: if you touch the surface with your finger you can feel the raised drops. This technique is mainly used for outdoor billboards. The image is not easily influenced by weather and is highly colour fast.

Thermal wax and dye-sublimation printers

Thermal wax printers use a plastic foil roll, the full width of the printer, printed with alternate wax-based ink stripes in the colours CMYK. When tiny elements mounted on a heating roll are heated, they cause the wax to melt and a dot of ink to transfer to the paper. Because the inks are not liquid, the printed result is often sharper in appearance than an inkjet result, but the high cost of the ink rolls makes these printers rather expensive to use. They also require expensive special paper. For colours other than the basic CMYRGBK, thermal wax printers need to use dither patterns, just like the inkjet printers.

COLOUR BASICS FOR GIS USERS

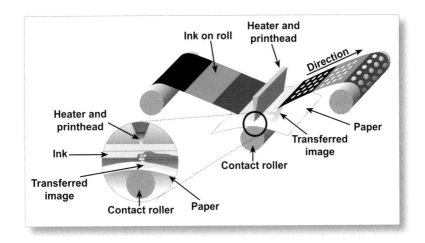

Figure 5.16 Principle of a dye sublimation printer

To overcome this problem, a variation of the technology has been created called dye sublimation. In this type, the heating causes the ink first to turn directly into a gas, i.e. to sublime, then to transfer to the paper and once there turn back into solid form. The amount of ink that sublimes, and therefore that transfers, is controlled by the amount of heat applied. If each heating element can have 256 different temperatures, then there are 256 corresponding transfer levels per ink, resulting in a possible 16.8 million colours, without dithering (Figure 5.16). These printers give photo-realistic quality but at a high price. The printers cost more than inkjet printers and the ink rolls are very expensive. Because of the slight spreading of the gas as it transfers, very fine lines do not print sharply.

Another problem is the registration of colour. For every colour the sheet of printing paper is transported back and forth. The starting point of the paper has to be exactly the same for all the four colours. High temperature is used to evaporate the ink and this also affects the dimensions of the paper, since heat causes the paper to expand. When printing photographic-type images any slight misfit does not show, but when printing thin lines and text it does show. This means that this type of printer is very well suited for printing image maps, but less for printing maps with linear information and text. The size of the printer is limited to a maximum of A3, at the present stage of development.

Laser printers

Laser printers are the most accurate of the desktop printers and tend to produce the best results. A low-powered laser diode (usually not a real laser) is used to 'draw' the image on a photosensitive drum, in the form of a positive charge. These areas pick up negatively charged particles of toner, which then transfer to the paper and are bonded by a heater (fuser) (Figure 5.17). The process is repeated for each of the colours CMYK. Colour laser printers are very expensive, but they are generally the fastest and produce the highest image quality.

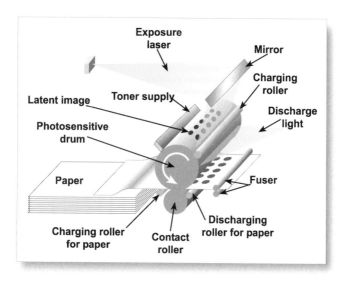

Figure 5.17 The principle of a laser printer

In recent years, several manufacturers have developed digital printing presses based on laser technology. These can print in formats larger than A3 and directly from a roll of paper. In business terms, they fill the gap between colour laser printers and the offset printing presses described in the next section. In a sense they compete with the digital offset presses and they focus on the printing on demand market, where every single printed sheet can be completely different from the previous printed sheet. These laser-technology presses are much used for personalised commercial brochures. Different types of digital printing presses are being developed and more information can be found on websites such as URL 5.14.

Offset printing

If you require many copies of a map, then offset printing is the most economical method. The fixed costs (and time) required to make an offset print are high compared to the variable cost per print, so that printing only a few copies is expensive. The exact 'cut-off' point below which offset printing is uneconomical compared to other printing methods is changing rather erratically because of improvements in the technology. The colour printers described in the previous section are becoming cheaper and faster, so tending to raise the cut-off point. On the other hand, improvements in offset printing technology and especially the introduction of digital offset printing are tending to lower the cut-off point. In making the decision as to which printing technique to use, many factors need to be taken into account, including format, type of paper and any special colour requirements (e.g. Pantone colours). For a few, small format CMYK prints one of the printing methods described earlier will usually give acceptable results; in all other cases it is best to seek professional advice.

Basic principles

The basic principle was discovered in Germany at the end of the 18th century. A special kind of limestone was used, hence the original term 'lithography'. A greasy image was first drawn (mirror reversed) on the polished flat stone. The stone was then dampened with water that did not adhere to the greasy image, only to the bare stone. A greasy ink was applied with a roller. The ink adhered to the greasy image but not to the damp bare stone. Paper was then pressed against the stone and the ink image transferred to the paper.

This was a slow process, and several major improvements were soon introduced. Using light sensitive coatings, methods were found by which a grease-receptive image could be formed on the stone by light exposure to an original image on film. The heavy, costly stones were replaced by thin sheets of water-receptive metal (first zinc, later aluminium) that could be bent round a cylinder, so increasing the speed of printing. The pressure of the paper tended to wear away quickly the image on the printing plate, so a transfer cylinder was introduced with a rubber blanket wrapped around it. The ink image transfers (or 'offsets') to this blanket cylinder, and then transfers again to the paper. This technology remains widely used today, and it is shown diagrammatically in Figure 5.18. A typical printing press consists of a combination of printing units one after the other, very often four, each unit printing a different colour in perfect fit (register) on to the same sheet of paper.

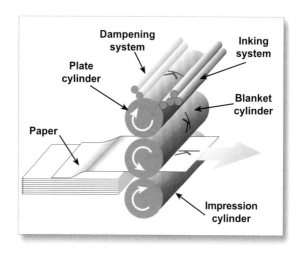

Figure 5.18 The principle of the offset printing press

Offset printing has major advantages:
- very fast (up to tens of thousands of sheets per hour);
- can print very fine lines and small text in any colour;
- large formats are possible.

The technique also has disadvantages, however:
- the method can produce only ink areas or non-ink areas (so, not a grey from black ink);
- the machines are extremely expensive and require skilled manpower to operate them;
- the cost of plate making and the 'make-ready' time is the same no matter how long the print run, therefore it is not an economical printing method for only a few copies.

COLOUR BASICS FOR GIS USERS

Technical developments (such as direct-to-plate systems, automatic registering, computerised inking systems and automatic cleaning) are reducing the preparation time drastically and therefore also lowering the minimum number of sheets at which offset printing can compete in cost with other printing systems.

Tint and halftone screens

In the early days of offset printing more than forty printing plates could be required for a geological map, for example. This was very time consuming and costly. The technique of screening was introduced in order to reduce the number of plates. Production methods were for many decades entirely analogue, required skilled craftsmen and were rather slow. A percentage tint screen consists of a plastic film covered by rows of very small dots, commonly 54 or 60 per cm. The rows (lines) of dots are often measured in inches, for example 133 lines per inch (lpi). After several processes using so-called 'masks' and light-sensitive emulsions the tint screen dots are reproduced on the printing plate in only the areas desired. When these dots are reproduced as ink dots on white paper, the eye sees a tint of the colour (i.e. colour plus white) since the individual dots are too small to be seen (Figure 5.19, also Figure 2.8). The percentage area covered by ink governs how dark the tint appears.

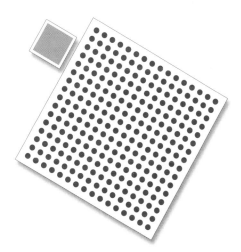

Figure 5.19 A screen tint

Figure 5.20 Halftone screening at two different screen rulings

A slightly different technique, halftone screening, was introduced to produce continually varying tints, as for the reproduction of photographs. Here, the size of the dots varies from place to place (Figure 5.20). The rather coarse screens used for pictures in newspapers can reproduce less detail than the fine screens used in high quality printing.

If screened images are printed one on top of the other using CMY inks, the result is a very large number of possible colours from only three printing plates. This is the principle of trichromatic or process-colour printing (see also Chapter 2). Because these screened images consist of a regular grid array of dots, you must take care that the angle between two screens is not too small or too large. If it is, the result is a so-called moiré pattern (Figure 5.21).

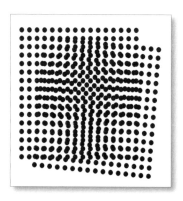

Figure 5.21 Moiré pattern

COLOUR BASICS FOR GIS USERS

When using regular screens with regular round dots, the difference in angle between the screens has to be exactly 30°. This allows for three colours only. When four colours are used, as in CMYK, some moiré is inevitable. To make this least obvious, this minimum moiré involves yellow, so the angles for the rows of dots are typically 30° for Y, 15° for C, 45° for K and 75° for M. Figure 5.22 shows how tint screens of different colours are printed on top of each other at the different angles. A pattern is visible, but this is a tiny rosette rather than a moiré. The standardisation of the differences in angle was actually fixed for the types of screens used in the pre-computerised film and printing plate production period.

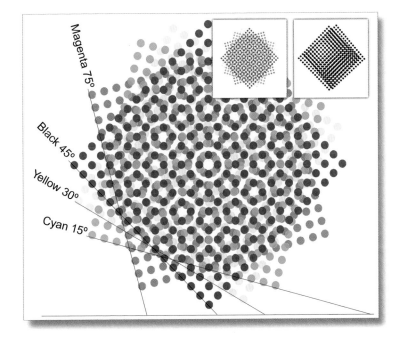

Figure 5.22 The angles of screen tints to avoid moiré patterns

Imagesetters

In the days of analogue technology percentage tints or halftone screened images were produced photographically; now they are produced using a computer. Still, mostly, a photographic film is required as an intermediate to produce the printing plate. This film is made using an imagesetter. With the aid of a Raster Image Processor (RIP), an imagesetter splits the image up into the four process colours (and if required in one or more additional spot colours) and prints each colour on to a clear film, with the correct dot sizes at the correct angles. The new techniques have removed the restrictions of a fixed dot shape for all colours, a fixed number of screen lines per inch and fixed angles of $30°$ between each colour. For example, a widely used DTP package (QuarkXPress) gives the following combination of screen lines and angles, for output on film for offset printing.

C:	126.492 lpi	$71.565°$
M:	126.492 lpi	$18.435°$
Y:	133.334 lpi	$0°$
K:	142.422 lpi	$45°$

An imagesetter has a very high resolution, at least 1200 dpi. 2400 dpi imagesetters are also much used and even higher resolutions are possible. A 2400 dpi imagesetter can produce a maximum of 95 dots per mm. These very small dots are produced on photographic film by extremely short exposure with a very fine laser. The colour of the laser and the colour sensitivity of the photographic film are closely related. During exposure the film is transported in the length direction, while the laser head moves back and forth over the width of the film. The dot resolution in width can be specified by the operator, up to the maximum. The resolution in the length direction depends on the speed of the film transport, but will generally be the same as the resolution in the width direction. It will be obvious that the higher the chosen resolution, the more dots have to be plotted and the more the RIP has to calculate. The tiny imagesetter dots are too small to be printable on an offset press, but they combine to make bigger dots that are printable.

A high resolution with small printing dots means that fine details are shown better. The higher the resolution of the imagesetter the higher the number of different tints that can be generated. Each dot of a percentage screen tint or of a halftone image on the final film is made up of the smaller dots produced by the imagesetter. Adding an imagesetter dot to a screen dot to make it bigger will cause a significant change in size if the imagesetter dot is itself relatively large. In this situation, therefore, only a limited number of percentage tints could be produced. Imagesetters can also produce what are called 'stochastic screens'. In this type of screen, the screen dots are small, all the same size, but arranged irregularly. Their density determines the percentage tint (Figure 5.23). The advantage of this type of screen is that it eliminates the possibility of moiré, so enabling more than four screened images to be superimposed. Standard process colours have difficulty reproducing very light colours, since there is a minimum printable dot size (about 8%). Adding very light versions of C and M (Y is anyway light) solves this problem, but is only possible with stochastic screens.

Figure 5.23 A colour from the ITC colour chart, made up of stochastic screen tints

Digital offset printing

The technology of offset printing is continuing to develop. One recent improvement is to produce the image directly on to the plate, without having to go through the film production stage. The term 'digital offset printing' is used to refer to two different techniques like this, both leading to final prints on paper. The first technique is strongly related to the traditional 'plate consuming' offset printing technology; in the second the removable plate is replaced by an image cylinder.

In the first type, the offset printing press is connected to a DTP system with a software RIP installed. The file to be printed is processed to a four-colour separation. Inside the printing press a Direct-to-Plate system transfers the digital image directly, by means of laser exposure, to an aluminium plate located in a drum inside the press. For each colour a separate plate is exposed, so the printing press has four plate drums and inking units. After producing the plates the machine can start printing. In this system no films are used. There is, however, no control mechanism to check the printing plates. Mistakes are only discovered after printing. After finishing printing, the used plates are rolled into another drum for waste plates, and a fresh plate is there ready for exposure. The big advantage of such a press is the short plate-making and make-ready time and the reasonable quality. Size is at this moment the bottleneck, but as for all applications that demand a lot of computer power, this restriction can change rapidly.

The second type of digital printing has been developed by the company Indigo [URL 5.15]. This is a type of electronic printing that evolved from electrophotography and offset printing. It combines the technology of digital data, laser imaging, and traditional offset printing. An Indigo press resembles a conventional offset printing unit. There is an image cylinder (like a conventional plate cylinder), a blanket cylinder that transfers the image to the paper (or other material) and an impression cylinder that supports the paper while ink is transferred to the sheet. One big difference is that only one unit does the actual printing.

The first step in the process is to load the processed raster data into the machine's main image memory. Next, the data are transferred to the laser imaging unit (writing head). The first image separation is imaged onto a Photo Imaging Plate (PIP). The plate is developed 'on the fly' using an elecrophotographic process and a patented ink (ElectroInk). The ink image is transferred to a special blanket that in turn transfers 100% of the ink to the sheet. The next image is made in the same way. It can use a different ink from the first image. The ink colours are conventional CMYK with the option of adding two additional colours. Compared to conventional offset printing the images produced are brilliant, sharp and of high definition.

This system can do things that a conventional offset press cannot do. It allows a different image with each print, which is ideal for personalised business mail. For each rotation, a different colour can be imaged, transferred to the blanket, and then to the paper. For a multicoloured print, successive coloured images are created on the PIP so the paper, therefore, makes four (or more) revolutions around the same impression cylinder. This is very different from conventional lithographic presses, which print only one image and one colour per unit. Because there is no plate-making and make-ready time, the system is economical for much smaller print runs than conventional offset. Registration, i.e. colour fitting, is easy since the paper sheet does not have to move from one printing unit to the next. At present, however, conventional offset is cheaper for long runs.

Output to digital files

When PCs really started to penetrate the office and general market, people assumed that paper consumption would drop as everyone started to transfer information electronically. This assumption was strengthened with the appearance of the Internet. Printing companies began to fear unemployment. The source for the fear of the printing industry was that most Internet users would download their information from the Web to their monitors. The number of Internet users would only increase, so, at a certain moment, hardly any information would need to be printed. That this prediction has proved to be wrong is fortunate for the whole hardcopy output business. Many office workers and Internet users want paper copies of the information they need. Also, the general printing of books, magazines and newspapers does not seem to be declining; there is still a big demand for these traditional products.

All the data found on the Internet are digital, prepared in such a way that they can be viewed on a monitor. They can also be printed. The same applies to digital files available in products like electronic atlases on CD-ROM, or the files produced by GIS software, word processing software or graphic software. In this chapter, we will focus on graphic files.

Types of files and formats

Vector

Vector images are collections of device-independent mathematical descriptions of graphical shapes. Vectors are line segments minimally defined as a starting point, a direction, and a length. They can, however, be much more complex and can include various sorts of lines, curves, and splines. Straight and curved lines can be used to define geometrical shapes, such as circles, rectangles, and polygons, which then can be used to create more complex shapes, such as spheres, cubes, and polyhedra.

Vector files are subject to change when interchanged between one software package and another. Shape and position are not affected but colour, form, style, etc., may change according to the demands of the user. Like bitmap files, vector files can contain palettes. Because the smallest objects defined in vector format files are the data elements, these are the smallest features for which colour can be specified. A rendering application must therefore look up colour definitions in the file palette before rendering the image.

Some vector files allow the definition of enclosed areas, which are considered outlines of the actual vector data elements. Outlines may be drawn with variations in thickness or styles. Enclosed elements may be designed to be filled with colour by the rendering application. The fill is usually allowed to be coloured independently from the element outline. Thus, each element may have two or more colours associated with it, one for the element outline and one or more for the fill. Fill colours may be transparent, for instance, and some formats define what are called colour attributes. In addition to being filled with solid colours, enclosed vector elements may contain hatching, shading or other types of patterns which are in turn called fill attributes. Certain vector file formats allow a geographical coding of elements, as well as adding attributes to each element or area.

Most graphic software packages have their own internal (native) file format, not readable by other packages. Often packages have a kind of internal conversion software, named 'import filters', to enable them to import files produced by other software. 'Export filters' enable a software package to save the file in an external file format. In order to be able to exchange data among packages or platforms some general exchange formats have been developed. Some of the more common vector formats are DXF, HPGL, PICT, SVG and WMF (see Glossary: Vector file formats).

Raster

Unlike vector data, in raster files the colour of each pixel is set for a certain purpose and is usually not meant to change. For more detail on how colour is described for raster files, refer to Chapter 4. Commonly used raster formats are Bit-mapped Graphic, GIF,

JPEG, PICT, PNG, TIFF and WMF (see Glossary: Raster file formats). Most of the raster file formats mentioned are usable on different platforms in different software packages. The TIFF format is the most widely used format when using DTP packages for final page make up. GIF, JPEG and PNG formats are used for exchanging files on the Internet.

Files for output to hardcopy and/or softcopy

In the past, when producing a map with the aid of the computer, the intention mostly was to generate a hardcopy on film or paper. Nowadays the hardcopy is not necessarily the final step and a map can be intended to be used in several ways. Of course a hardcopy is still an option, either on film to be offset printed, or directly to a printer. Printing a hardcopy can be done directly from within the software, using the simple 'print' command. If the colour management of the production line is well implemented, the outcome of the printed file will have the expected colours (Chapter 5).

Printing can also be done indirectly, i.e. your file has to be printed on a device that is not directly linked to your computer. The output device may not even be housed in your own organisation. To be able to print a file externally, outside your office, there are different options. The easiest is to copy the native file on a disk, together with all elements such as images and fonts, and give or send it to the graphic bureau that will produce the output. Files that are not too large may be sent by e-mail. In this situation the outputting bureau needs to have the same software available. Sending a PostScript file gets over this restriction, since all professional graphic bureau will be able to handle PS files. A disadvantage is the difficulty of editing a PostScript file, so a mistake can only be corrected with difficulty, if at all. It is worth noting that not every software package is capable of generating a good, 'clean' PostScript file, even if it claims to be able to!

Often a map or other graphic will be a part of another bigger document, e.g. a map in a report. The word processing software used to write the report cannot produce maps. The simplest way to put a map into a report is to rasterise it and place it as an image in the final document. Care has to be taken with the choice of pixel size: if the pixels are too large, details are lost, while if the pixels are very small the data file becomes very large. Rasterisation may also result in the loss of colour information. Better is to generate an EPS file. This file can be imported into another document and then printed on a PS printer. All information about colour, fonts, etc., is contained in the file and there is still the option of re-scaling and even embedding it in another EPS or PostScript file.

Most people are used to a print on paper and seem to have more confidence in printed matter then in the digital display. Slowly this attitude is changing and digitally displayable files are becoming more popular. They can be sent directly to one or more receivers by e-mail or made widely available over the Internet. In the editing process in the graphics industry it is now common for digital files to be seen and altered by many different people without any intermediate hardcopies being made. The simplest way to prepare a file for transmission and direct viewing on a monitor is to rasterise it into a format such as GIF, JPEG or PNG. The advantage is that the quality of the product can be set beforehand, including the colour use and resolution. Both elements influence the file size. When preparing a file for use on the Internet, the size of the file is very important, since the smaller the file, the faster the delivery. Small files mostly require a reduced number of colours and a reduced resolution, both of which have an influence on the readability of the map.

A logical step in the development of file formats was the Portable Document Format (PDF), developed by Adobe on the basis of the PS format and now a widely accepted *de facto* standard. Conversion to PDF from a document in another format is done using commercial software, Adobe Acrobat. To read PDF files on a PC monitor, Adobe Acrobat Reader software is required. This is downloadable free of charge via the Internet [URL 5.16]. In a PDF file the original layout is maintained, as well as the use of colour, fonts, etc. Extra elements such as hyperlinks or indexes can be added, which makes it more than just the digital equivalent of the printed map. As with PostScript, you can zoom in without losing detail. On the contrary, zooming in reveals more detail, since the vector image is rasterised for screen display on the fly. The International Colour Consortium (ICC) standardised colour management systems can be included, so there is control over the final output [URL 5.17]. One big advantage of PDF over PostScript is that corrections can be done in the file even if the mistake is discovered just before printing. A PDF file that is viewed on a PC monitor has already been interpreted by Acrobat Reader from the original file. It can therefore be printed directly on any printer, automatically at the resolution of the printer. It is now becoming common practice, for example, to distribute bulky documents such as software manuals in the form of PDF files on CD-ROM. The PDF files are rather compact and are ideal for publishing all kinds of information over the Internet.

Internet files

Most computer platforms have a minimum standard 256-colour palette for displaying images, but most modern PCs can display millions of colours, depending on the graphics board that is used. When preparing images for display using an Internet browser, however, it is recommended to use the Web Safe palette, since you never can be sure which system the user on the other side of the line has available (for a detailed description of this palette see Chapter 6).

File size is important for graphics on the Web. Internet data are transmitted over telephone lines and via modems, both of which have limitations concerning data volume and speed of transmission. Users do not like having to wait for a long time for a graphic image to appear. Depending on the type of graphic, one can often make do with many fewer colours, therefore smaller colour depth, therefore smaller file size.

Maps can combine linework, area fills, text and raster images. Lines in a map and also the text are vector-based; they are described mathematically. This makes them resolution independent, i.e. they can be scaled to any size and resolution for display on screens and for printing. These vector files are smaller than the raster files of comparable graphics, so they are very suitable for use on the Internet. The PDF format has already been described. Macromedia Shockwave is another much used format. Scalable Vector Graphics (SVG) is a standard described by the World Wide Web Consortium [URL 5.18]. SVG is likely to be widely used on the Internet in the near future.

In order to view files in these vector formats, the Internet user must (at present) download so-called plugins. To play safe and avoid this requirement the vector file can be converted into a raster image. Either the software in which the map is produced

---

has export filters for this or the map first can be exported as an EPS file and afterwards rasterised by using image processing software. For use on the Internet, the formats mostly used are GIF (for purely vectors, areas and text) and JPEG (for continuous tone images like photographs or hill shading).

The disadvantage of a raster image is that lines appear jagged. This effect can be reduced by using the technique of anti-aliasing. This is the process of adding intermediate colours to smooth out the jagged edges between lines and areas of solid colour. Anti-aliasing improves the appearance of lines but adds more colours to the image and hence increases the size of the palette used. Therefore, if you want a high quality image, you may have no option but to increase the file size.

Colour management systems

In the graphics industry in general the problem is how to reproduce colour correctly. This can be the colours of a photograph or, even more difficult, the colour of an actual object, say a glass of cola in an advertisement in a magazine. In cartography and GIS we are more concerned with creating colours on a display screen and then reproducing them correctly on paper. In both cases, colour management systems can be useful.

If you start with hardcopy, say a photograph or a drawing, a scanner is needed in order to transform it into digital raster data. These data are then processed using computer software, often making use of a screen display, e.g. for retouching photographs and adjusting their colour. A proof hardcopy of the final result may then be made on a printer before going on to make the offset prints. Keeping good control of colour throughout all these processes is not easy.

The goal of colour management is to coordinate the colour spaces of all the devices involved to allow a data interchange that will guarantee a true-colour reproduction of images and graphics. It should be possible to ensure repeatable and above all predictable colour reproductions. Another aim is to make it possible for you to simulate one output process on another output device. For example, you should be able to imitate the final offset printed result on a display screen and on an inkjet printer.

The basic principle of colour management is analogous to the problem of grid reference conversions among different map projections. This is commonly done by converting a grid reference on the first projection to the corresponding latitude and longitude, then converting these values to a grid reference on the second projection. In colour management, all colours are described in terms of a device-independent colour space, usually the CIELAB space (Chapter 3). All that is required is then a transformation forward to and backward from this space for every device used.

This seems simple enough. However, a major problem is often that some colours that can be produced on one device are outside the colour gamut of another device. To solve this problem an adjustment has to be carried out in which, on the second device, the colour is found that is closest to the 'out of gamut' colour of the first device. At the same time, the overall impression and the relation of colours to each other have to be maintained, so the entire colour space has to be adjusted.

These complex operations are carried out by colour management software. To operate a colour management system, all the devices used have to be colour calibrated, to get what are known as device profiles. The manufacturers often provide these. Older devices may not have these profiles and also the colour characteristics of devices can change with time, so there has to be a way to calibrate devices.

A scanner is calibrated by scanning a special test document, the IT8 document, provided by the International Colour Consortium (ICC). This document contains about 250 different colours. The result of scanning will give the device-specific colour values for each colour. The software provided then prepares a conversion table to relate scanned values to the original document values, e.g. CIELAB values, and it derives the equations that link one with the other. This is the device profile.

Calibration of a monitor involves using a special measuring instrument very similar to a spectrophotometer, that can be attached to the monitor with a small suction cup. The calibration software then generates a series of different colours that appear one after the other at the same spot under the measuring device. As for the scanner, the device profile is calculated by comparing the measured values with the expected (theoretical) values.

To calibrate a printer you again need special tools. A test document provided in digital form is printed. The individual colour fields are then measured using a spectrophotometer and these measurements are used to calculate the device profile. Because a new set of ink cartridges may be slightly different from the old set, the printer should be re-calibrated when the cartridges are replaced. Also, you should calibrate for every type of paper you use. You can generate a device profile for an offset printing press in exactly the same way, although here you first need to output the test document on an imagesetter. In the case of a printing press, the profile is known as the print table.

Colour management depends on all the device profiles being accurately known. The process is obviously simpler if the entire production procedure is standardised, using the same devices, inks and paper. Nevertheless, it remains a somewhat complex operation and the measuring tools and the software together are expensive. Large graphic companies can justify the cost but it is a different matter for the often small organisations that work with GIS. For them, a much simpler approach is possible, based on colour charts.

Chapter 6

Colour charts

The use of colour charts and palettes

A colour chart is a set of different colours, usually ordered and displayed in some logical way. It is used to guide colour selection. Printing ink manufacturers, for example, produce colour charts or fans showing all the colours they can supply. A colour chart may indicate the 'recipe' for each colour. The Pantone colour fan (Chapter 2) does just this, so that the offset printer knows exactly which of the basic colours have to be mixed together in which proportions to get the desired colour. Colour charts displayed on a flat surface such as a monitor screen or paper may be based on a three-dimensional colour order system such as the Munsell or Ostwald system (Chapter 3).

Printed colour charts may be based on spot colours but most commonly they use percentage tints of the process colours CMY, with the possible addition of black (K). On a computer monitor all colours are produced using additive RGB. Many graphic software packages contain colour charts of RGB matches to Munsell, Pantone and other colours but, as explained in Chapter 2, the result can never be more than an approximation. When a map or other GIS display will be viewed only on a computer monitor it is better to use a colour chart or colour selection system that uses RGB directly. These charts and systems are usually based on a colour space such as the cube or the HLS or HSV spaces described in Chapter 3. These spaces may offer a very large number of colours, e.g. 16.8 million. The user has to navigate within the space in order to select colours. Depending on the system and software configuration, it may be possible to choose among a number of standard colour palettes or lookup tables (LUTs) containing a smaller number of colours (Chapter 5).

It is very important to realise that if the computer monitor is set to display only 256 colours, then many of the colours in most of the above-mentioned palettes will appear dithered. The exception will be the standard palette for the computer system, e.g. the Windows palette. However, a standard palette in one system will not appear smooth if displayed on another system set to 256 colours, e.g. the Windows colours will not appear smooth on a Macintosh computer and vice-versa. Yet limiting the palette to 256 colours has the big advantage that it can greatly speed up computer processing and also reduce file size. This is especially important for the Internet, when data have to be transferred over telephone lines.

The Web Safe colour palette

Because the Internet is supposed to be usable by a wide variety of computer systems, a rather simple 256-colour palette had to be designed which would give smooth, non-dithering colours on all systems. The Web (or Browser) Safe colour palette (the printed version of which is reproduced in Figure 6.1) has been accepted as the industry standard [URL 6.1]. But note that the palette will only appear smooth when you are using the Internet. If you copy Internet files into some other software the colours will appear dithered, unless you set the display to 24-bit colour (or 32-bit 'True Color').

The basic idea is a colour cube with six intensity steps, including zero, along each of the RGB axes, resulting in 216 (i.e. 6^3) colours. The main problem users have with this is the hexadecimal colour notation, in which a typical colour code could be #CCFF33. All the colours have a six-character code like this. As explained in Chapter 4, the hexadecimal system uses base-16. This has the advantage that, since $256 = 16^2$, 256 intensity levels of RGB (i.e. one byte per colour) are each represented by a two-digit number. The full code for a colour therefore occupies less space than it would in the decimal system. The six intensity steps used by the Web Safe colour palette have the levels 0 (written as 00), 33, 66, 99, CC, FF, in hexadecimal notation. Their decimal equivalents are given in Table 6.1.

Hexadecimal	Decimal	Hexadecimal	Decimal
00	0	99	153
33	51	CC	204
66	102	FF	255

Table 6.1 Web Safe colours

COLOUR BASICS FOR GIS USERS

000	003	006	009	00C	00F	030	033	036	039	03C	03F
060	063	066	069	06C	06F	090	093	096	099	09C	09F
0C0	0C3	0C6	0C9	0CC	0CF	0F0	0F3	0F6	0F9	0FC	0FF
300	303	306	309	30C	30F	330	333	336	339	33C	33F
360	363	366	069	36C	36F	390	393	396	399	39C	39F
3C0	3C3	3C6	3C9	3CC	3CF	3F0	3F3	3F6	3F9	3FC	3FF
600	603	606	609	60C	60F	630	633	636	639	63C	63F
660	663	666	669	66C	66F	690	693	696	699	69C	69F
6C0	6C3	6C6	6C9	6CC	6CF	6F0	6F3	6F6	6F9	6FC	6FF
900	903	906	909	90C	90F	930	933	936	939	93C	93F
960	963	966	969	96C	96F	990	993	996	999	99C	99F
9C0	9C3	9C6	9C9	9CC	9CF	9F0	9F3	9F6	9F9	9FC	9FF
C00	C03	C06	C09	C0C	C0F	C30	C33	C36	C39	C3C	C3F
C60	C63	C66	C69	C6C	C6F	C90	C93	C96	C99	C9C	C9F
CC0	CC3	CC6	CC9	CCC	CCF	CF0	CF3	CF6	CF9	CFC	CFF
F00	F03	F06	F09	F0C	F0F	F30	F33	F36	F39	F3C	F3F
F60	F63	F66	F69	F6C	F6F	F90	F93	F96	F99	F9C	F9F
FC0	FC3	FC6	FC9	FCC	FCF	FF0	FF3	FF6	FF9	FFC	FFF

Example of colour code: code nr. C39 indicates hex. nr. CC3399

Figure 6.1 The Web Safe colour palette

The colour code given at the start of this section, namely #CCFF33, therefore indicates a colour consisting of 204R + 255G + 51B, in decimal notation.

The extra 40 colours (256 minus 216) in theory available on a system set to 256 colours are not in fact displayable on all combinations of computer, monitor and graphics board. Where they are displayable they are used for the ten missing intensity levels of grey and of R, G and B alone, on a 16-step scale. Using the hexadecimal notation these levels are 11, 22, 44, 55, 77, 88, AA, BB, DD, EE. Their respective decimal equivalents are 17, 34, 68, 85, 119, 136, 170, 187, 221, 238.

It must be remembered that, although the Web Safe palette contains 216 colours, some of these colours are very similar to each other. This tends to be the case more with PCs using the Windows operating system than with Apple Macintosh computers [URL 6.2].

The significance of this colour palette for users wanting to use the Internet to send maps and other graphic images is that only the colours of the palette are guaranteed to appear smooth, or 'flat'. If you have prepared a map using graphics or GIS software and you have used combinations of RGB that do not appear in the palette, then one of two things will happen in the receiver's Internet browser, if the system is set to 256 colours. The browser may select the palette colour closest to the one you have used or else create a dither pattern of the closest colours. From a distance the dithered colour will appear similar to the one intended but at closer viewing the pattern will be clearly visible. In practice nowadays, website designers tend to assume that all users have systems capable of displaying 24-bit colour (i.e. 16.8 million colours) so they do not feel restricted to the Web Safe palette.

Printed colour charts

Printed colour charts on single sheets are limited by the format of the paper they are printed on. The colour squares on a chart have to be big enough to be a reliable guide to colour selection so the number of colours contained is always limited. The most important thing to bear in mind is that the chart should be produced using exactly the same technology and printing equipment as used for the final printed map. Only by so doing will it be a reliable guide to colour selection. The charts we will consider further in this chapter are those in which percentage tints of different coloured inks are overprinted, so as to produce many colours from few printing inks.

When designing a printed colour chart, the following questions have to be answered:
- Which printing inks to use?
- How many percentage tints?
- Which percentage tints?
- How to arrange the chart colours on the sheet of paper?
- What is the perceptual influence of neighbouring colours on each other?

An offset printed colour chart can be made using any printing colours. The number of overprinted colours is limited to three (or four) to avoid moiré, unless you are using stochastic screens. Let us take the example of topographic maps. These are usually printed using a set of perhaps six spot colours, e.g. black, blue, red, brown, green and yellow. Especially for area colours, the map designer will want to use tints of the individual colours and possibly some combinations, e.g. tints of yellow and red combined to make orange. To make a choice he will want charts in which tints of two or three of the printing colours are combined. Map types such as geological, soil and vegetation maps often require a very large number of colours. A common system is to start with six to ten spot colours and make a colour chart combining tints of any two of these. For example, using six printing colours, seven tints of each (excluding white paper, including full colour) plus the combinations of any two will result in 777 chart colours, excluding white paper.

Most printed colour charts, however, use the trichromatic system, i.e. process colours. These are especially useful for GIS users since monitors and printers also use the trichromatic system, in the additive and subtractive versions respectively. The rest of this section will deal with printed charts produced using combinations of CMY(K) inks. In the days of analogue map production the map designer was restricted to using a limited range of percentage tints available on plastic film. Nowadays the use of computer technology allows any percentage tint of each of the process colours to be used. Colour charts still serve a useful purpose, however, by establishing fixed points to use as the basis for interpolating the colours in between.

The more tints you use in the chart, the larger the number of colours. However, there is a limit to the number of colour squares you can get on one sheet of paper. Also, all the colours are contained by the same colour space, therefore the consequence of a large number of colours is very small differences between adjacent colours, so small that the difference may be hard to perceive. For these reasons the number of tints is usually limited to five to ten.

Which percentage tints to choose is a difficult problem. A common aim is to try to get equal appearing steps from white to the full colour. The difficulty is that steps that appear equal by one method of printing may appear very unequal by another. Also, the steps might appear more or less equal for a single printing colour but not for combinations of colours. These problems are dealt with in some detail in the next section of this chapter.

Colour charts using CMY are very often based on the colour cube, 'sliced' to reveal the colours inside. Figure 6.2 shows a colour cube based on Figure 3.13, using the CMY tint equivalents of the Web Safe palette (with no colour management applied).

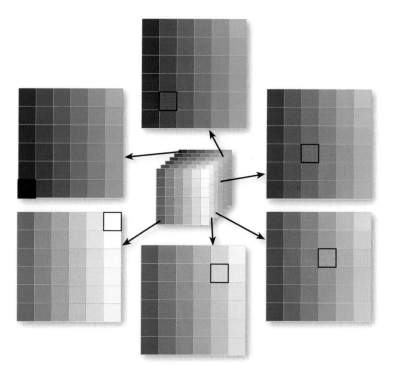

Figure 6.2 A Web Safe colour cube in slices (grey scale highlighted)

It can be seen that these tints are not ideal for maps: the steps do not appear equal. Furthermore, there is a preponderance of dark and rather highly saturated colours whereas cartographers like also to use light and pale colours.

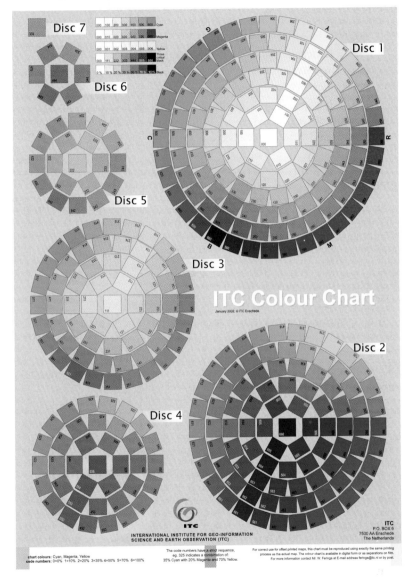

Figure 6.3 The ITC colour chart

This very simple cubical arrangement is not intuitive. If you want to use a lighter and a darker version of the same yellowish-green hue, for example, it is not at all obvious how to do this. This is the reason why graphic software packages use more intuitive colour spaces such as HLS or HSV rather than the cube. It is possible to do something similar with printed charts. The colour chart (Figure 6.3) used for many years by the authors at the ITC is derived from an arrangement of colours that is similar to the HLS system (and also to the Ostwald system). The chart uses five intermediate tints between zero (white) and 100% (solid colour), resulting in 7^3 chart colours, i.e. 343 colours including white. A PDF version of the chart can be downloaded from the website accompanying this book (http://kartoweb.itc.nl/colour).

As explained further in Chapter 7, the same colour can appear different if the background or neighbouring colour changes. Also, colours against a white background tend to appear dark. To avoid these effects, the colour squares of the ITC colour chart are not immediately adjacent to each other, but are separated by a medium grey background.

Printing and measuring screen tints

Before going on to discuss the ITC colour chart in detail, the results of printing percentage tints on paper need to be examined. These results had a major influence on the selection of tints used in the chart. In Chapter 5 we have seen that there are many different techniques by which a coloured image can be printed on paper. If they are not using a colour management system, cartographers and GIS users may be unpleasantly surprised when a particular printer does not produce the colours they expect, or when an offset printed map looks quite different from the inkjet printed version. One major reason for this is that the hues of the CMY inks in use by the different systems are not exact matches and therefore the gamuts do not match. Another reason is that the offset printed version may use only CMY whereas the inkjet or laser printer will automatically add K. Furthermore, tints are not produced in the same way by the different systems. In offset printing they are made by overprinting screen tints of CMY. Inkjet printers on the other hand produce tints by printing semi-random patterns of CMYK dots.

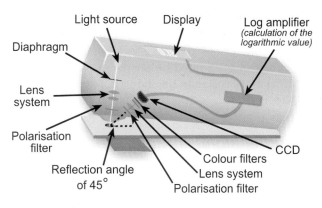

Figure 6.4 A typical densitometer

One method of examining these effects is to print the same tints by different techniques and then to measure the result. A readily available measuring instrument is a densitometer as used by offset printing personnel (Figure 6.4). Photographic or printing density is defined as follows:

Density = log (1/reflected (or transmitted) light)

A grey ink that reflects 10% of the light reaching it has a density of $\log(1/0.1) = \log 10 = 1$
A black ink that reflects 1% of the light reaching it has a density of $\log(1/0.01) = \log 100 = 2$

A typical densitometer can be calibrated so that the white paper has a density of zero. It can also measure percentage tints, for which the full, solid colour is calibrated to 100%. When measuring the densities and percentages of CMY inks, the corresponding RGB filters are used. In theory, solid cyan should transmit no red, so should appear black through a red filter. Similarly, magenta appears black through a green filter and yellow appears black through a blue filter. If no filter is used, the densitometer just measures the 'grey' value, i.e. the lightness of the colour. The examples given here are the results of measurements carried out on the ITC colour chart reproduced by different printing techniques or using different paper. In these examples only the lightness of the chart colours was studied, hence no filter was used for the measurements. The densitometer was calibrated absolutely, not to each paper sheet separately.

The different printings measured are as follows:

1. A3 format chart offset printed on uncoated paper (as reproduced at smaller size in this book in Figure 6.3, but on different paper)
2. Chart colours printed using an A4 HP Color LaserJet 5m printer on uncoated paper
3. Chart colours printed using an A4 HP DeskJet 890C inkjet printer on uncoated paper
4. Chart colours printed using an A4 HP DeskJet 890C inkjet printer on glossy, 'photo quality' paper

The DeskJet printer used allows many parameters to be set by the user, in particular regarding colour management. For the prints used for measurement no colour management was used since this ensures that in a series of tints of magenta, for example, no dots of other printing colours are added.

The original intention in choosing the percentage tints for the ITC colour chart was that the perceptual differences between adjacent tints of the tint scale should appear equal. The corollary is that the central tint should be perceptually central between the end points. However, as already mentioned, a set of tints that achieves this by one printing method may not do so by another printing method. Furthermore, although you may get a satisfactory result for tints of a single ink, the result of combinations of two or more inks may not be so good.

The ITC colour chart was first designed with offset printing in mind, using overprinting of conventional screen tints of CMY. At that time, using analogue production methods, tint screens were only available in steps of 5%. Research at the time showed that the following tints produced a reasonable approximation to an equal-step scale: 0%, 10%, 20%, 35%, 50%, 70% and 100%. These steps were given the code numbers 0 to 6 on the chart, always in the sequence CMY for each chart colour. The central tint, 35%, is unexpected: you would expect 50%. This is because printed tints on paper are much darker than the tints on the film used to make the plate. The reasons are firstly that the ink dots spread (a process called dot-size gain) as they are transferred to the paper and, secondly, that so-called internal reflection by the fibres of the paper make tint areas darker than expected. The first effect depends very much on the amount of ink and the pressure applied in the printing press; the second effect depends mostly on the type of paper. Paper that has been given a chalky coating has less internal reflection: it is therefore preferred for high quality printing. Most maps, however, are printed on uncoated paper.

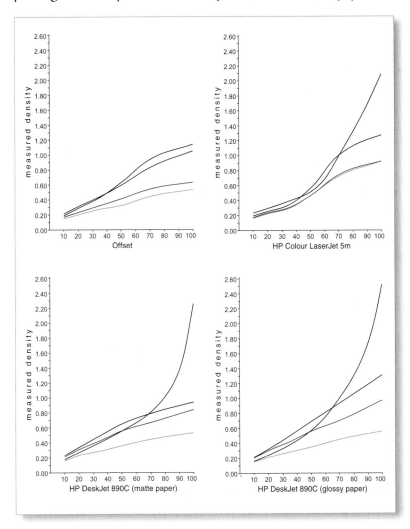

Figure 6.5 Tints of cyan, magenta, blue (C+M) and black printed by different techniques

The version of the ITC colour chart that was measured was produced digitally. One major change compared to the analogue version is that so-called stochastic tints are used. The coloured dots are distributed at random instead of in rows, so avoiding any possibility of moiré patterns on the printed result. This printing of the chart was done on a different press than earlier printings. The result shows that the intended equal-step lightness scale has not quite been achieved in that the 70% tint appears a little too dark. However, as shown in Figure 6.5, some of the other printing methods produce somewhat better results.

The printed chart colours can be compared in several ways. A very simple method is to plot on a graph the measured densities of each tint of each printing colour and then draw a curved line to connect the points. In Figure 6.5 yellow is not included because even solid (100%) yellow is not much darker than white paper. In three of the graphs magenta is shown to be darker than cyan. Blue is always darker than cyan or magenta, since it is produced by overprinting the same tints of these two inks. The most striking thing about the graphs of Figure 6.5 is the behaviour of the black ink. On the offset printed chart the black curve has a similar general shape to cyan, magenta and blue. On the inkjet and laserjet prints the plotted curves for black slope sharply upward for the darker tints, especially for 70% and 100%. This is evident on the printed tint scales as a very large perceptual step from the 50% tint to 70% and again to 100%.

It is possible to measure tints on an absolute scale of density and at the same time to find out if there are significant differences in the perceptual steps between adjacent tints in any scale. To do so we have to refer back to the Munsell colour system (Chapter 3). Munsell designed his system based on the average perception of many observers. His grey scale has perceptually equal steps. These greys can be measured using a densitometer. Munsell allowed space at the end of his scale for a 'whiter' white and a 'blacker' black. Standard white paper has a Munsell grey value somewhere between 9 and 9.5, while the printing process is unlikely to produce a black with grey value much below 2.5. In the graphs of Figures 6.6 and 6.7, Munsell grey values are plotted on the x-axis (reading from high to low, from 9.5 to 2) and densities are plotted on the y-axis. The curved line is then the Munsell grey scale. Densitometer measurements of greys darker than 2.5 are not very reliable, hence this part of the curve is shown as a dashed line. The next step is to use this graph to indicate perceptual differences. This was done for two colours on each of the four printed versions of the ITC chart colours: blue (C+M) in Figure 6.6 and black in Figure 6.7.

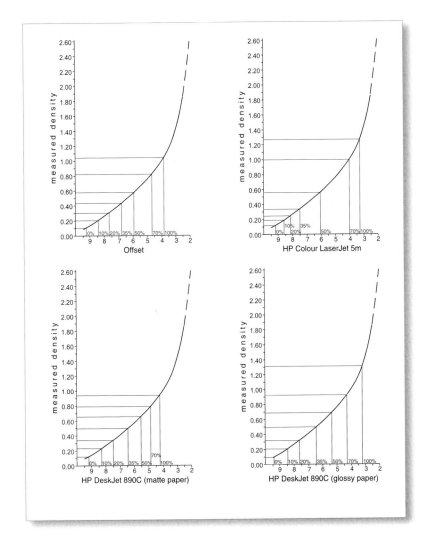

Figure 6.6 Tints of blue (C+M) printed by different techniques, plotted on the Munsell density curve

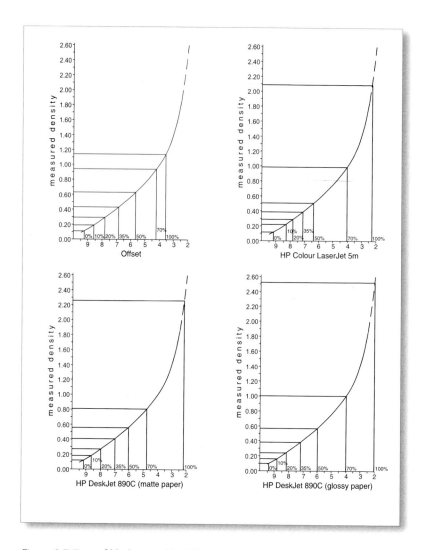

Figure 6.7 Tints of black printed by different techniques, plotted on the Munsell density curve

In each graph the measured densities of the tints used are plotted on the y-axis. By intersection of these values with the curved line of the Munsell grey scale, the corresponding positions on the x-axis are found. Equal distances on this axis represent equal perceptual differences. The graphs show that the full (100%) colour has a different density on different prints and that the perceptual scale of the tints used shows unequal steps. For both blue and black, the 70% tint on the offset printed chart is shown to be rather dark — a tint of 65% would give a better result. In Figure 6.6 the inkjet print on glossy paper shows the most nearly equal perceptual scale. For the inkjet and laserjet prints the graphs clearly demonstrate the anomalous behaviour of the black ink. This has a greater effect than might at first appear. In the offset printed chart all the colours are produced by tints of CMY only. In the inkjet and laserjet printers, K is automatically added to replace the grey component of a colour. In theory, a colour consisting of 35%C, 20%M and 70%Y would be printed in 20%K, 15%C and 50%Y, although in practice the grey component replacement involves more complex calculations, different for each type of printer. This system has some advantages, for example greater hue constancy and good neutral grey colours, but it does mean that the darker colours that are combinations of all three of CMY are very strongly influenced by the behaviour of the black ink and consequently appear very dark.

The Munsell graphs can of course be used in reverse to produce equal-step value scales. The first step is to print a long series of tints, say in 5% steps from 0 to 100%, using the printing method that will be used for the final map. The measured densities of each tint are then plotted on the y-axis of the Munsell curve. The required equal steps can then be plotted on the x-axis and the corresponding percentage tints interpolated on the y-axis. For offset printing this method can be applied to spot colours as well as to CMYK.

The procedure of measurement and comparison can be taken a step further, although at the cost of much time and effort. The principle is to produce a large number of tints and their combinations for each output device normally used. From densitometer measurements (using the filters) the colours are found that form the best match on different devices, probably taking the final offset printed result as the standard. Then, an appropriate LUT for each output device is made, so that the output on each will appear more or less the same. This method can never be more than an approximation to a true colour management system, however.

The ITC colour chart and its properties

Many of the decisions made when the ITC colour chart was originally designed have already been explained above. Figure 6.8 shows a colour cube containing 343 colours (including white paper), made from tints of 10%, 20%, 35%, 50%, 70% and 100% of CMY. This cube can be transformed into a double cone with white at the top, black at the bottom and 100% CMYRGB arranged around the largest circumference (Figure 6.9). This double cone clearly has a close affinity to the HLS and Ostwald

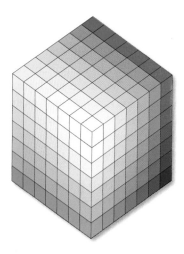

Figure 6.8 A CMY colour cube

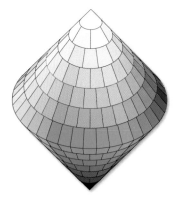

Figure 6.9 The cube transformed into a double cone

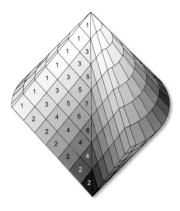

Figure 6.10 The interior of the double cone

systems. Figure 6.10 shows a section cut out to reveal the interior. For the ITC colour chart the solid is 'exploded' into conical shells and each shell flattened out to make a disc consisting of concentric circles of colour squares. The numbers in Figure 6.10 refer to the numbers given to each disc in the chart. Figure 6.11 shows the arrangement of one printing colour (cyan) for the largest disc, number 1. If you cut out disc 2 of the chart and place it on disc 1 you will see that they actually share the outermost colour circle. This is printed once only to save space, however. The same is true for discs 3 and 4 and for discs 5 and 6.

Each colour square of the chart is given a unique code number referring to the percentage tints of CMY, in that sequence, that make up the colour. Code 0 refers to 0%, 1 to 10%, 2 to 20%, 3 to 35%, 4 to 50%, 5 to 75% and 6 to 100%. For example, colour square with code 436 consists of 50%C + 35%M + 100%Y. Figure 6.12 shows part of the A3 size printed chart, with code numbers. If, as intended, the perceptual steps from one tint to the next in the printed chart are indeed equal, then tint 4, for example, is seen as twice as dark as tint 2 and four times as dark as tint 1, all of course with the same hue. The same is true for tint ratios, so, for example, colours 012, 024 and 036 all have the same hue. They therefore all lie on the same radial line, in this case in disc 1 of the chart. In theory, colour 222 is grey (in practice not quite), so colour 246 can be thought of as 024 + 222, or 024 plus grey. Colour 246 has, therefore, the same hue as colour 024. It can be found in disc 2 in exactly the same relative position

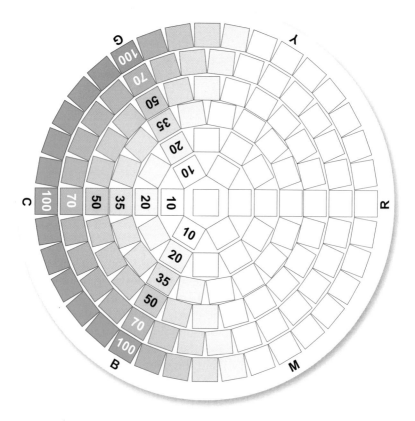

Figure 6.11 Tints of cyan in ITC colour chart disc 1

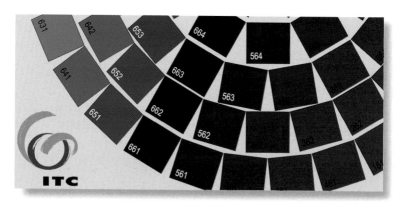

Figure 6.12 An excerpt from the full-size ITC colour chart

as colour 024 in disc 1: the two colours have the same chroma as well as the same hue, differing only in lightness.

This arrangement of colours has several useful properties.

- The hue angle or azimuth indicates hue: same angle, same hue, on any disc. Diametrically opposite hues are complementary. The colours of the grey scale are to be found at the centres of the discs. Note that due to grey component replacement, these theoretical properties work better in practice on inkjet printed charts than on offset printed charts.

- Colours become darker downward in the colour solid. Hence in the chart the colours of discs 1, 3 and 5 become darker outward, while the colours of discs 2, 4 and 6 become darker inward. Notice that, just as for the HLS and Ostwald systems, colours in any one circle do not have the same lightness.

- Chroma increases outwards: very approximately, you can assume that all colours at the same distance from the centre of any disc have the same chroma. Colours with the same chroma all have the same difference between the lowest and highest numbers in the colour code, e.g. colour 623 has the same chroma as colour 154. A vertical line drawn through the solid will pass through colours with the same hue and chroma, differing only in lightness.

- The colours close to the centre of the solid are close to medium grey. Further away they are lighter, darker or more saturated. All the colours of disc 1 have at least one of CMY as 0%, all colours in disc 2 have at least one of CMY as 100%.

It is also possible to imagine the double cone sliced vertically, as is done for the Ostwald system. Figure 6.13 shows vertical slices for the complementary hue pairs C-R, M-G and Y-B. For each of these six hues there are 21 variations in lightness and chroma. You will find that there are fewer variations for other hues. This is a consequence of the fact that the chart is based on a transformed cube rather than on a true HLS or Ostwald system. For digital map production, however, the percentage tints of CMY for the 'missing' colours can be interpolated. For example, you can assume that colour 0%C, 35%M, 15%Y lies perceptually midway between chart colours 021 (0%C, 20%M, 10%Y) and 042 (0%C, 50%M, 20%Y).

Just as in the HLS and Ostwald systems, absolute position in relation to the central axis of the colour space does not have a

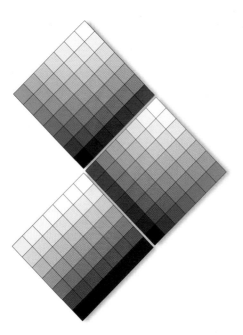

Figure 6.13 Variations in lightness and chroma for the complementary pairs C-R, M-G and Y-B

direct relation to lightness. Lightness can be judged approximately by eye, also in relation to the grey background of the chart. For more accuracy, the lightness of each colour can be measured using a densitometer, without coloured filters. These measurements can then be put into a lightness table.

The arrangement of the colours in the chart, together with the lightness table, allow colours to be selected following some systematic principle. For example, two colours with the same hue and chroma but different lightness must lie on a vertical line in the colour solid, so on the chart they will be in exactly the same geometric position in different discs. Colours that differ in hue but have the same chroma and similar lightness are equidistant from the centre of any disc and close together in the lightness table. 'Clean', rather bright colours (no colours being combinations of all three of CMY) are to be found in disc 1; somewhat duller, but not dark, colours in disc 3; very dull colours in discs 5 and 6. Some further hints on colour selection principles, also using the ITC colour chart, are given in Chapter 7.

Chapter 7

Hints on the use of colour on graphic display screens and printed maps

Why use colour?

Map makers use colour for two reasons.

- Colour is one of the available visual variables, and if carefully used can greatly improve the communicative quality of the display.
- Colour can be applied as an aesthetic element to improve the appearance and graphic quality of the map or display.

Perceptual and psychological factors influencing colour choice

Perception psychologists have found several factors concerning the human perception of colour, relevant to map makers (Robinson, 1967). Some of the more important ones are given below.

- With decreasing size of symbols hue differences become less easy to perceive.
- With increasing area, the apparent saturation and chroma of a specific colour increase.
- The eye is more sensitive to small lightness changes than to small hue changes.
- One of the basic eye-brain mechanisms is to enhance contrast between adjacent objects. Thus, two almost similar hues adjacent to each other can more easily be distinguished than when they are separated from each other. Also, a particular colour will appear lighter if seen against a dark background and will appear darker against a light background.
- Specific hues have specific human associations, e.g. 'warm' colours such as orange and red, 'cool' colours such as blue and turquoise; red for danger, green for safe; blue water.

These factors translate into some particular recommendations, which apply to screen displays and printed maps.

- If you have small point symbols or thin line symbols, make sure they have very distinctive hues compared to each other and to the background colours. The use of value differences improves distinctiveness.

- Do not judge selected colours to be used for area symbols only from small colour squares on a colour chart; always test them on the map. Be especially careful with yellow, large areas of which can easily be too dominant, despite it being a light colour even at high percentages.

- Area symbol colours that are fairly similar in hue and lightness may be difficult to tell apart on the map. To increase distinctiveness it is better to slightly change the lightness of one of them rather than to slightly change its hue.

- Two colours that appear reasonably distinct when adjacent in a legend may appear indistinguishable when separated on the map. The same colour may appear different in different parts of the map, according to the surroundings, so you may not be able to relate map colours easily to legend colours.

- Colour associations have given rise to cartographic conventions. Familiar conventions include blue water features and green forest areas on topographic maps. In a thematic map containing both positive and negative values it is common to use warm colours for the positive values and cool colours for the negative values. Some conventions arise from colour dominance and colour contrast, e.g. red for main roads. Other conventions are based on an arbitrary choice, e.g. the standard colours used for geological maps. The topic of conventions is dealt with in more detail later in this chapter.

Colour choice for screen displays

There are three main ways in which graphic screen displays are used for spatial data visualisation and interaction in a GIS and in geoinformatics in general:

- as interactive working documents in a GIS (for exploring and analysing data), in digital photogrammetry and in digital image processing systems;
- as final presentations, with or without user interaction;
- as the design phase for producing paper maps and graphics.

Interactive working documents

Vector and raster formats may both be used, possibly simultaneously. The main criterion for colour use is that important information should be shown by colours that are as distinct as possible from each other. When working with vectors it is common practice to use a black screen background, not white. This has two advantages: a black screen cannot flicker, and light colours, e.g. yellow, stand out better than on a white background.

Raster images may simply be scanned from paper maps, aerial photographs, etc. It is important that these images have sufficient contrast and distinct colours, but it is usually not necessary to match exactly the colours of the original document. Where necessary, contrast and colour can be manipulated using a standard graphic image processing package such as Photoshop.

Sometimes the raster image must be manipulated as part of the data exploration and analysis procedure. This is especially the case in digital image processing of satellite data. These data have no inherent colour: colours are introduced as part of the image processing. You may want to display either a coloured, photographic type of image or else the result of a classification procedure. In the first case you may combine images of different wavebands or from different sensors in order to produce an image which has 'realistic' or 'false infrared' colour or one in which colour differences are manipulated to aid visual interpretation (Figure 4.8). In all cases, you will probably want an image with the maximum possible colour differences. This is done by transforming the colours used so that they fill as much as possible of the RGB colour cube while still maintaining their internal relationships. The transformation methods involved are beyond the scope of this book: they can be found in textbooks on digital image processing of remotely sensed data (e.g. Dury, 1993) or in articles in scientific journals (e.g. Pohl and Van Genderen, 1998). In the case of classifications, there are colour conventions that can be applied in many branches of the Earth sciences. This topic is dealt with in more detail below.

Raster images that represent real or statistical surfaces are a special case. Each pixel has a z-value and these z-values are represented by a colour scale. The simplest is the grey scale. The highest contrast is achieved when the lowest values are black and the highest values are white, or vice versa. Another type of colour scale has hue as the main differentiation factor. One commonly used scale begins at dark blue then rises through light blue, green, yellow, orange, light red to dark red: this is the so-called 'spectral' scale. Cartographers may not be very happy with this scale, since it does not follow a recognised theoretical principle such as 'the higher the darker'. It does, however, have the advantage that z-value zones are clearly distinguished from one another, which is useful during data exploration and analysis. Many digital image processing packages include a variety of default colour scales from which the user can select.

If possible, it is a good idea in any exploration or analysis task to reserve the high chroma colours for the data in which you are really interested. Other data, or background data, may be shown by low chroma colours, or even by shades of grey. For example, if you are not at all interested in water features, then show rivers in black or dark grey, lakes and the sea in light grey. If you use a bright blue for these features, you are simply distracting your attention from the important data. In some software packages this principle is used when vector data are overlaid on a raster background, or for screen digitising from a scanned image. The background can be made to go pale, simply by automatically adding white pixels, while darker and high chroma colours are used for the vector data.

Final presentations on display screens
Final presentations of maps on display screens include TV weather maps, map displays for in-car navigation systems, computer games, atlases on CD-ROM and maps sent over the Internet. These examples illustrate one common feature, namely that the creator of the map does not have full control over the final appearance: much depends on the colour settings of the user's display and on the adjustment of brightness, contrast and colour balance. One result of this can be, for example, that two colours that appear sufficiently different to each other on the creator's display may not appear so on the user's display. Furthermore, if the user has his display set to 256 colours his system may select the nearest available colour or attempt to match the desired colour by dithering.

A good deal of research has been done into colour use for screen displays for various special purposes, for example for day and night versions of electronic charts for use on a ship's bridge

[URL 7.1]. The main design aims include the creation of a display that is unambiguous even on poorly adjusted monitors while also being quite restful to the eye. Note that if the display is too brilliant, i.e. uses high chroma colours, the user will soon become tired. When designing a display yourself, for example for use on the Internet, it is always advisable to view it as intended (in this case, after being sent over the Internet), and to view it under unsatisfactory conditions, e.g. high ambient light, badly adjusted monitor. As in all map design, much depends on the experience and skill of the designer.

Designing paper maps on display screens

In Chapters 2 and 5, the problems of matching a display screen to final paper output have been discussed in detail. The main thing to remember is that the design should be made with the final output in mind and tested using that output. If you have a good colour management system you will achieve something close to WYSIWYG, 'what you see is what you get'. In this case you can select colours on the screen and be sure that the final printed result will have very similar colours. Colour management systems are too expensive for most GIS users, however, so they will have to work with colour charts, as described in Chapter 6.

Colour choice for maps

When designing a map you must always consider the technology that will be used to produce it, how it deals with colour and what colours it can produce. The fundamental principles that apply to the selection of colours for use on maps, especially those that will be used to present information to other people, are that the colours should follow some kind of logical system and that there should be some relation between the colours used and the information being presented. Generations of cartographers have developed guidelines for the use of colour (Robinson et al., 1995). Many GIS users are, however, not trained cartographers. Especially for them, the most important guidelines are given here.

Colour conventions

These have already been mentioned in this chapter. Early maps were often hand coloured but the widespread use of colour on maps began in the second half of the 19th century, with the development of lithographic plate-making techniques based on light-sensitive emulsions. Some familiar conventions date from that period and the early 20th century, for example in topographic mapping the use of blue for water features, green forest areas, brown contours and red main roads. Also in that period the geologists broadly standardised their use of colour and other Earth sciences followed. Because these conventions have become so familiar, they assist the user greatly, since he needs to refer less often to the map legend. So the guideline here always is to follow existing conventions unless you have strong reasons for not doing so.

Sometimes these conventions conflict. A good example is the use of green for vegetation conflicting with the conventional representation of relief on small scale maps by means of layer colours in the series dark green, light green, yellow, light brown, medium brown, dark brown and purple (see Figure 7.11 for a typical set of conventional layer colours). The layer colour (or tint) convention was developed in north and central Europe and eastern North America, where it fits the landscape with its green, cultivated lowlands and bare, brown mountains. However, it does not suit the landscape colours in many other parts of the world, where for example a low-lying desert may be fringed by green, forested mountains. In these areas the desert has relief layer green on the map, while the mountains are brown. The conflict is obvious. Conflicts like this can to some extent be avoided by the application of more advanced cartographic theories on the use of colour that make systematic use of the variables hue, lightness and saturation (or chroma).

The use of hue

The variable hue is used to identify map features and to differentiate between features that are different in type, i.e. have a nominal or qualitative difference. You can think of this as a kind of colour coding. In order to show related features, you can use colours that have hue angles close together in the Munsell, Ostwald or HLS colour spaces, or in the ITC colour chart. For example, you may want to use different green hues to represent different types of forest.

On some maps you may want to select hues that are as perceptually distinct as possible. The higher the saturation or chroma of the colours the greater the perceptual differences

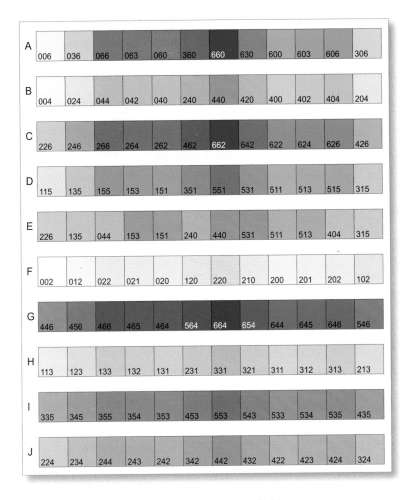

Figure 7.1 Variations in lightness and chroma in a set of 12 hues

between colours with the same angular difference in the colour
spaces just mentioned. This is one of the reasons why many GIS
users like to use high chroma colours in a screen display. On a
printed map, however, these colours are not restful to the eye.
Figure 7.1 demonstrates that inter-colour discrimination becomes
less as chroma decreases. The figure shows variations of the
same set of 12 hues, equally spaced in the ITC colour chart.
The biggest inter-colour differences are to be found in row A,
consisting of colours with maximum chroma, all situated in the

outer ring of disc 1 of the chart. Although the angular spacing of the colours in the disc is constant, the actual perceptual differences are not: colours in the red-magenta area appear rather similar in hue, for example. As in all symmetrical double-cone colour spaces, the colours in any one ring do not have the same lightness. The colours in rows B, C and D are taken from the fourth ring of discs 1, 2 and 3 respectively. They all have the same medium chroma. Row E contains colours taken from rows B to D, selected to minimise the lightness differences. Rows F to J of the figure consist of colours of low chroma taken from the second ring of discs 1 to 5 respectively. The perceptual difference between adjacent colours in these rows is small.

Many colour conventions are actually hue conventions. In the case of geological mapping, for example, there are a great many conventional colours. Where there are many colours on one map, in order to make sure that they remain distinct you will find that you have to use the variables lightness and chroma as well as hue. As mentioned earlier the use of warm and cool hues to express positive and negative values respectively is a common convention, also the use of red for danger, as in hazard mapping.

The use of lightness

Lightness can be used to represent relative importance or order, or numerically classified data, for use in area symbols or large point symbols. The general guideline is 'the more the darker'. Note, however, that the saturation and chroma will also change in such scales. For example a tint scale of red chosen from the ITC colour chart could use all six steps from 10% (code 011) to 100% (code 066) from disc 1. In this scale, as the colours become darker (i.e. the lightness decreases) the saturation and chroma increase. If you now go on and add black, i.e. by choosing colours in the red direction from disc 2 (166, 266, etc.), the colours continue to become darker as you go towards the centre of the disc, but the chroma now decreases (Figure 7.2A). For a long lightness scale, using these darker reds may be unavoidable, but it is better in this case not to use the high chroma, 100% red in the centre of the scale since this may tend to dominate the map visually.

If you have a numerical classification with many steps, you will find that the steps may not be sufficiently distinct if you use only the variable lightness. Much also depends on the printing method used – in the example of Figure 7.2A some of the darker colours may appear very similar to each other when printed on an inkjet printer. If there are more than about six steps, it is better to introduce hue differences as well as lightness differences. In population density maps, for example, it is common to begin with very light yellow then progress through darker yellows, oranges and reds to dark red or brown. These colours form a spiral arrangement in the ITC colour chart solid with the central colours in the scale being of higher chroma than the colours at each end (Figure 7.2B). It is not easy to create a long lightness scale with hue shift but no change in chroma. Figure 7.2C is a short scale of this type using only the colours present in the fourth rings of discs 1, 2 and 3 of the ITC colour chart.

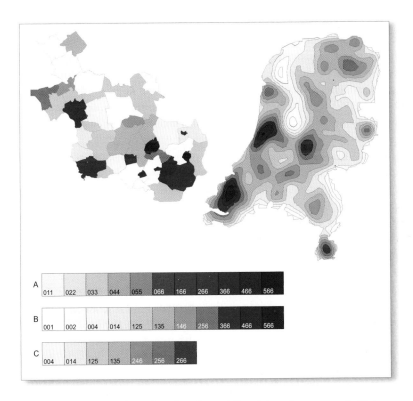

Figure 7.2 Lightness scales with no hue change (A), with hue change (B) and with hue change but constant chroma (C). Scale B used on a choropleth map (left) and on an isopleth map (right).

Numerical classifications are used for two types of area symbols: choropleth and isopleth. The first type is based on administrative areas, for example a population density map showing the density per municipality. The second type is based on the concept of a classified statistical surface. If you want to make a rainfall map, for instance, you collect data from weather stations, treat these as z-values and calculate the surface that best fits the z-values. By 'contouring' this surface you create the isolines. To make the pattern more easily visible on the map, it is common practice to fill in the areas between the isolines with the appropriate colours from a lightness scale, in this case usually in the hue blue. For maps like this based on a statistical surface, the colours on the map always appear in the same sequence as in the legend. Because of this, you can use very long lightness scales on isopleth maps and still get a legible result, even though the differences between adjacent steps are small. On a choropleth map, on the other hand, any colour may be adjacent to any other on the map. In the case of choropleth maps, therefore, the scales should be short, maybe with only four to six steps. This is even more necessary if the choropleth map includes some very small areas, when as we know, human colour discrimination is poor. In the case of infill for numerically classified data in possibly quite small proportional circles, it is also necessary to use a short scale of lightness. Figure 7.2 shows the same 11-step lightness/hue scale used on two maps, a choropleth map and an isopleth map (both using imaginary data). Comparison with the legend colours (Fig 7.2B) is easier from the isopleth map.

Layer tints used to represent relief are an example of surface mapping. So here you might expect 'the higher the darker'. In fact this is often done. It is also possible to modify the conventional layer tints to follow this rule, e.g. by beginning at very light green and ending at dark brown, with a gradual change in hue and lightness in between (Figure 7.3). In the mapping of ocean depths, it is common to use the hue blue, with the rule 'the deeper, the darker'.

On some maps there may be both positive and negative lightness scales, for example maps showing net immigration or emigration. In these cases, as already mentioned, it is common to use warm yellows, oranges and reds to represent net positive values and cool greens, blues and purples for negative values. Temperature maps

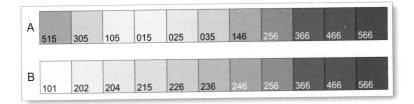

Figure 7.3 Conventional layer tints (A), modified to follow the rule 'the higher the darker' (B)

are interesting in this respect. Zero degrees on the Centigrade scale is an arbitrary temperature, yet it is common to see on maps darker cool colours for below-zero temperatures and darker warm colours for above-zero temperatures (see Figure 1.3).

The use of saturation and chroma

These variables could in principle be used like lightness to represent ordered or numerically classified data, but they have tended to be used less than lightness for this purpose. Experiments have also been made to use chroma to represent uncertainty, with the most certain data being represented by colours of highest chroma (Brown & van Elzakker, 1993). In the commonly used tint scales described in the previous section, saturation and chroma are anyway involved: both increase with higher tint percentages to a maximum, then chroma (but, strictly speaking, not saturation) decreases again towards the very dark colours. A colour scale in which the only variable is chroma has at one end the high chroma colour and at the other a grey of the same lightness. Using only the colours of the ITC colour chart it is not easy to create such a scale without introducing changes in lightness also (Figure 7.4A).

If the graphic software allows, it is also possible to create chroma scales using black ink and a coloured ink (Figure 7.4B).

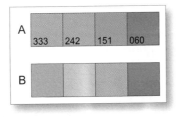

Figure 7.4 A chroma scale of magenta, using CMY (A) and magenta plus black (B)

When printed by an inkjet printer both versions will appear similar because the printer will replace the grey component with black ink, but when printed by offset (used for this book) there is a clear distinction – the grey produced by CMY is not a neutral grey.

As mentioned earlier, high chroma is often used to draw attention to important information, or vice versa, low chroma is used for the least important information. If you do not want any information to be dominant, then use colours which have rather similar, medium chroma and avoid colours of very high chroma, like the colours in the outer circle of disc 1 of the ITC colour chart. Be especially careful with yellow in this respect. One difficulty with chroma is that the apparent chroma and saturation increase with area, so that a medium yellow that looks quite inoffensive on the colour chart dominates the entire map if used for a large area.

Colour aesthetics

So far in this chapter, the emphasis has been on the systematic use of the colour variables in order to improve the communicative quality of the display. Most map makers, however, also want to create a map that looks attractive. The production cost is not higher and an attractive design encourages the user to study the map. In some branches of cartography, for example road and tourist mapping, design is a very important factor influencing map sales.

There are a great many factors that influence the graphic quality of a map and one of them is colour. An artist is also very interested in colour and cartographers can learn a lot from artists. On maps, however, the positions and areas of features are fixed, unlike in a painting, where the artist can control the composition. This makes the cartographer's job in some ways more difficult than the artist's. However, even people with little artistic talent can produce reasonably attractive maps if they follow a few basic design rules. These rules are of course in addition to the guidelines on the use of colour for good communication, already discussed earlier.

The map should appear nicely balanced. Great care should be taken in the use of dark or very high chroma colours, especially for area symbols. In general, complementary hues form good colour matches. For example, a map with area symbols in green colours and point symbols in magenta colours is likely to appear well balanced.

Psychologists talk about the 'figure-ground' relationship. The ground is the background information, represented on maps by pale tints or greyish colours. The figure is the important, foreground information, represented by dark or high chroma colours. A figure-ground relationship that is well supported by the colour choice should appear attractive and easy to read.

Sometimes map designers try something unusual to attract attention to the map theme: for example using a scale of reds to indicate water pollution. There is always room for experiment. The appreciation of the aesthetic aspects of colour is influenced by cultural and age differences. People with a certain cultural background may have a preference for soft colours, others may prefer bright colours. Children also tend to prefer bright colours.

Examples of colour use

If you are using a GIS, you may not want to spend too much time on colour selection: you may be quite happy with one of the defaults offered by the system or else with a standard set of colours in use in your organisation. Possibly, however, you will not find a default set that suits you so you will have to create your own colours. Much depends on what you want to use colour for. If you are analysing data you may want to create extreme colour differences in order to make spatial patterns and correlations more obvious on the colour monitor, or you may want to emphasise certain data by using very high chroma colours. If on the other hand you want to present your results in maps and graphics in a printed report to be read by people who are less deeply involved in the subject matter than yourself, then you should select colours very carefully so that they support the subject, appear to have been chosen logically and produce an easily readable result. The following examples illustrate these principles.

Nominal area data

Map types that represent nominal area data are called chorochromatic maps. They include common types such as maps of geology, soils, vegetation and land use. In these maps, hue is the basic colour variable that is used, but it should not be applied in a 'random rainbow' fashion. The map in Figure 7.5 shows the

---

land use of the central area of a city. The red of most of the blocks is very dominant but still some other colours stand out, especially the yellow, the two greens and the very dark grey in the bottom left corner. You might assume that these represent very important categories of land use. There are two blues, dark and light: presumably these represent different categories of water. After some time you notice that there are orange city blocks among the dominant red ones: presumably these represent a land use category of less importance than the red blocks. The colours as a whole are rather brilliant and not very restful to the eye.

Figure 7.5 Urban land use

This map in fact includes some typical faults that can be made if colours are not chosen correctly. Most of the colours have high chroma, which accounts for their brilliance, and also explains why the yellow stands out so strongly – it is lighter than most of the other colours as well as being of high chroma. The strong red represents residential use and the less dominant orange represents commercial use. Yet you would probably expect the commercial use to be represented as more important than the residential use, so to be more dominant on the map. The very dark grey at the bottom left is part of the airport. Is this land use really so important? The medium green for recreational use (parks, etc.) seems reasonable, but the dark green has nothing to do with vegetation, representing as it does industrial areas. Dark blue is in fact water, as expected, but the light blue represents transport land use. Of the remaining colours, yellow represents institutional use and medium grey is used for vacant land. The conclusion is that the colour choice for this map can be improved.

When you set about choosing colours more systematically for this map, you can ask yourself four questions.

- Which land uses are most important, which least?
- Which land uses are related?
- Are there any widely accepted colour conventions I can use?
- How will the colour balance appear on the final map and how easily readable will it be?

Even after you have answered these questions you will still find you have a good deal of freedom in colour choice. In consequence, the map in Figure 7.6 represents only one possible attempt at an improved representation. The basic assumption is that commercial, institutional, industrial and transport land uses should receive most emphasis so the colours used are dark and/or of high chroma. The airport is a transport use so should appear to be related to it. Blue for water and green for recreation are commonly used conventions, and there is no reason to depart from these. Grey for vacant land also seems to be a good choice. For readability and balance a very wide selection of different colours can be quite acceptable but it is best to use lighter or low chroma colours for less important information. In general it is also advisable to avoid high chroma colours for large areas.

Figure 7.6 Improved colour choice for urban land use

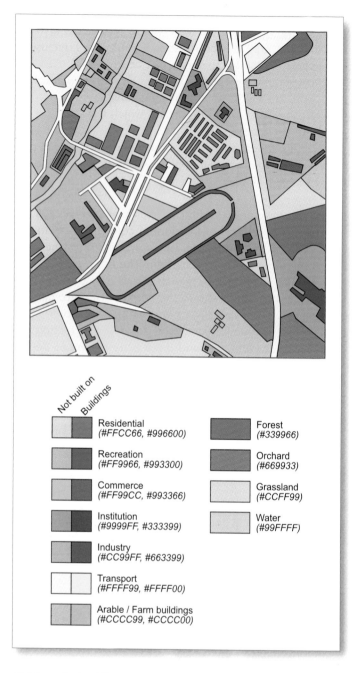

Figure 7.7 Hue and value differences in land use mapping (HTML colour codes in brackets)

Sometimes the different types of data in a chorochromatic map can be visually grouped by the careful use of the visual variables. The map extract with accompanying legend shown in Figure 7.7 is also a land use map. This map uses Web Safe colours (the HTML codes are given). The general principle is that hue is used for type of land use, with a darker tint used for buildings. This makes it easy for the user to distinguish the buildings at a glance, and still relate them to the land use type. Since forests and orchards also rise above ground level, fairly dark colours are used for these land uses.

It is possible to develop rather complex systems for grouping land use types. A problem that might occur, however, is that a carefully thought out system might not give such good results if something changes in the printing procedure. Figure 7.8 shows a simulation (in offset) of two versions of the same map legend, printed on the same inkjet printer, with and without using the colour management available in the printer software. The colours are taken from the ITC colour chart (codes in brackets). The ideas behind the legend structure are that crops on irrigated land should have colours of higher chroma than crops on non-irrigated land, and tree and shrub crops should both be rather dull, with

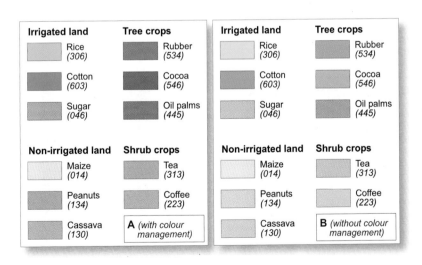

Figure 7.8 A complex scheme for land use colours (ITC colour chart codes in brackets). Left shows a simulation of an inkjet print with colour management, right without.

the tree crops being darker than the shrub crops. The figure demonstrates that it is especially necessary to test complex colour systems using exactly the same production method as will be used for the final paper print.

Classified numerical data: layer tints

Elevation data or more generally data representing a 'statistical surface' are very often used in a GIS. These may or may not be classified into distinct layers, with a colour applied to each layer. Figure 7.9 shows a representation of a digital elevation model that may be useful at the data analysis stage, using a monitor. There are distinct layers, with gradual colour variations within each layer, so that finding all regions with the same elevation is easy. This representation does not, however, follow Bertin's rules of cartographic semiology, according to which the representation of such data on a map should follow the rule 'the higher the darker' or 'the higher the lighter'. The second of these two rules is applied in Figure 7.10, using very narrow layer classes. The result gives a reasonable general impression, but because the only visual variable used is lightness it is not easy to compare elevations in different parts of the map. Furthermore, the greys tend to become rather dark on the printed version.

There are some strong conventions in colour use for elevation layer tints, for example as shown in Figure 7.3A. A typical

Figure 7.9 Distinctive layers for data analysis

Figure 7.10 A grey scale, 'the higher the lighter'

conventional colour series is used in Figure 7.11, with some topographic symbols added. In this region, the villages and therefore the roads are concentrated mainly at low elevations, but the dark green makes the symbols less legible. Furthermore, this convention does not follow either of the Bertin rules. In Figure 7.12 the rule 'the higher the darker' is applied, but with a gradual hue change from greenish yellow to brown, to assist in finding zones with the same elevation. The dense topographic information in the low ground is now clearly visible against the very light colours used there.

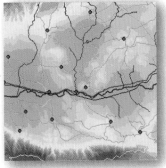

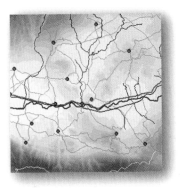

Figure 7.11 Conventional elevation layer tints

Figure 7.12 'The higher the darker' with gradual hue shift

Layer tints combined with hill shading

If you are using standard GIS software you will be able to represent elevation data by a variety of default layer tinting methods and you may be permitted to devise your own colour scheme. Commonly you will be able to display a Digital Elevation Model (DEM) also by hill shading, with an imaginary light source normally from the north-west. This gives an impression of the landforms. Sometimes you might want to combine these two methods of representing relief. In many parts of the world there is a strong correlation between altitude and slope: the greater the altitude the steeper the slopes. When combining layer tints with hill shading, in order to bring out the high contrast in the hill shading in the areas with steep slopes, i.e. the high elevation areas, it is best to use a layer tinting scheme following the general rule 'the higher the lighter'. However, the lower areas should not be too dark or the hill shading in these areas will not be clear and any other map symbols will be difficult to read.

The example given here illustrates these principles as well as showing two different technical approaches to combining the displays. In the first place a layer tinted display and a hill shading display were made from a rastêr DEM of a volcano in the Philippines. The layer tints go from medium green in the lowlands to light yellow at the mountain peak (Figure 7.13A). The version of the hill shading made from the same DEM, shown in Figure 7.13B, has high contrast. The DEM and the displays were created using ILWIS software. ILWIS, like some other GIS software packages, can also be used to combine the displays. The basic principle is to separate the layer tint display into its RGB components, then multiply each component by a variable factor based on the value of the hill shading display for each pixel. The resulting components are then recombined. The multiplication factor derived from the hill shading display has to be experimented with until a result is achieved that fits the intended purpose. Figure 7.13C shows one possible result.

If you have an advanced graphic image processing package available, such as Photoshop, the two images can be combined directly. The principle is to put the images in different layers and to make the top layer increasingly transparent in order to reveal more of the layer underneath until the desired result is achieved. Figure 7.13D, E and F show the layer tints overlaid by the hill shading, which has 20%, 40% and 60% opacity respectively. If you invert the layers to put the hill shading underneath and then vary the opacity of the layer tints on top the results appear noticeably different on the screen from the first case. However, on exporting from Photoshop to a TIFF file for printing, the results in both situations are identical, since the transformation to TIFF simply creates a proportional amount of each image, e.g. 40% of image X and 60% of image Y. This is a typical example of where you do not have as much control over the situation as you might like.

Figure 7.13C, produced by calculation within the GIS software, tends to maintain the chromaticity of the layer tints outside the heavily shaded areas. In the combinations D to F, produced using Photoshop, as the contrast in the hill shading is made to increase

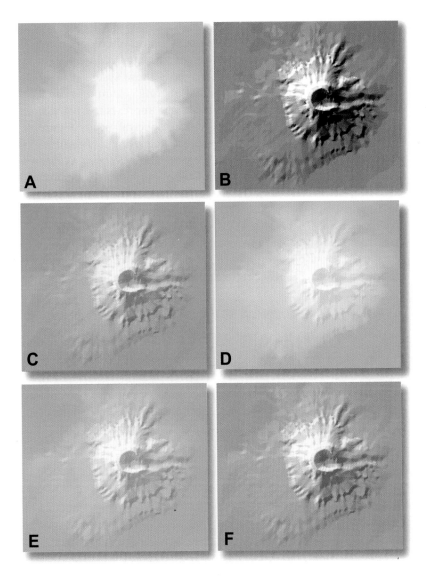

Figure 7.13 Layer tints, hill shading and various combinations of the two

by increasing the opacity of the hill shading image, the overall chromaticity of the combination decreases: the result becomes duller. Which of these (and of the many other possible) outcomes is preferred is partly a matter of taste.

Classified numerical data: use of HLS

GIS software packages often allow the selection of colours using the HLS or HSV systems or one of their variants. Many different types of colour scales can be created using these systems. Figure 7.14A shows the result of a distance buffering operation from roads carried out using ILWIS software and represented using one of the default colour scales available, the 'spectral' scale. Figure 7.14B shows the same data now represented using a chroma scale, from high chroma magenta to grey. The Microsoft Windows HLS system is used in which each of the variables has a maximum value of 240. In this case, the magenta hue (H) has value 200, the luminance (L) is fixed at 120 and the saturation (S) is made to vary in steps: 240, 180, 140, 100, 80, 60, 40, 30, 20, 10, 0. The saturation steps need to be adjusted until a satisfactory result is achieved, on the screen and/or on the printed map. The result printed in Figure 7.14B is certainly not the same as on the screen.

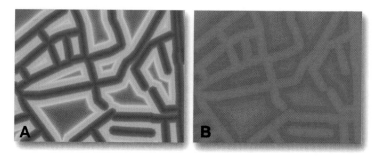

Figure 7.14 Two representations of a road buffering operation

Some conclusions

In this chapter, some of the most important principles relating to colour use on maps and in a GIS have been discussed and illustrated. Using colour spaces and colour charts, with some thought colours can be selected that actively support the theme of the map or graphic. The use needs to be borne in mind, considering also the differences between printed paper output and the screen display. Anybody who follows the general guidelines summarised in this chapter will be able to produce an acceptable, readable result from the GIS data and with the addition of artistic and design skills the result can also be made more attractive.

References

Berlin, B. & Kay, P., 1969, *Basic Color Terms: Their Universality and Evolution*, Berkeley/Los Angeles: University of California Press.

Bertin, J., 1967, *Sémiologie Graphique*, Paris: Gauthiervillars/ Mouton. [Translated by W.J. Berg and published in English in 1983 as *The Semiology of Graphics*, Madison, WI: University of Madison Press.]

Brown, A., 1993, Map design for screen display. *The Cartographic Journal* (Vol. 30, Dec. 1993), p. 135.

Brown, A. & van Elzakker, C.P.J.M., 1993, *The use of colour in the cartographic representation of information quality generated by a GIS*. Proceedings of the 16th International Conference of the International Cartographic Association, Cologne, Germany, pp. 707–720.

CIE, 1989, *International Lighting Vocabulary*, Vienna: publication No. 17.4, 1989.

DeMarco, P., Pokorny, J. & Smith, V.C., 1992, Full spectrum cone sensitivity functions for X-chromosome linked anomalous trichromats. *Journal of the Optical Society of America* (A, 9), pp. 1465–1476.

Dury, S.A., 1993, *Image Interpretation in Geology*, London: Chapman & Hall.

Hering, E., 1964, *Outlines of a Theory of the Light Sense*, Cambridge, MA: Harvard University Press. Translated by L.M. Hurvich and D. Jameson. Originally published 1920.

Luo, M.R., 1998, Colour science. In *The Colour Image Processing Handbook*, edited by Sangwine, S.J. & Horne, R.E.N., London: Chapman & Hall.

Palus, H., 1998, Colour spaces. In *The Colour Image Processing Handbook*, edited by Sangwine, S.J. & Horne, R.E.N., London: Chapman & Hall.

Pohl, C. & Van Genderen, J.L., 1998, Multisensor image fusion in remote sensing: concepts, methods and applications. *International Journal of Remote Sensing* (Vol. 19, No. 5), pp. 829–854.

Robinson, A.H., 1967, Psychological Aspects of Color in Cartography. *International Yearbook of Cartography* (7), pp. 50–59.

Robinson, A.H., Morrison, J.L., Muehrcke, P.C., Kimerling, A.J. & Guptill, S.C., 1995, *Elements of Cartography* (6th edn), New York: John Wiley & Sons, Inc.

Sangwine, S.J. & Horne, R.E.N. (editors), 1998, *The Colour Image Processing Handbook*, London: Chapman & Hall.

Shaw, M.Q., 1999, *Evaluating the 1931 CIE Color Matching Functions*, M.S. thesis, Center for Imaging Science, Rochester Institute of Technology, Rochester, New York. (PDF <www.cis.rit.edu/research/mcsl/research/mshaw/ CMF_Thesis.pdf>)

URLs

URL 2.1 http://www.pantone.com
URL 2.2 http://www.pantone.com/hexachrome/

URL 3.1 http://www.anthus.com/Colors/NBS.html
URL 3.2 http://www.anthus.com/Colors/Cent.html
URL 3.3 http://www.colordome.com/cla/ostwald/01ost01.htm
URL 3.4 http://www.ncscolour.com/
URL 3.5 http://www.adobe.com/support/techguides/color/
colormodels/munsell.html
URL 3.6 http://www.munsell.com/Download.htm
URL 3.7 http://www.it.lut.fi/research/color/demonstration/
demonstration.html
URL 3.8 http://www.colorsystem.com/projekte/engl/47dine.htm
URL 3.9 http://www.efg2.com/Lab/Graphics/Colors/HSV.htm
URL 3.10 http://www.efg2.com/Lab/Graphics/Colors/
Chromaticity.htm
URL 3.11 http://www.adobe.com/support/techguides/color/
colormodels
URL 3.12 http://www.ite.rwth-aachen.de/herzog/pages/
gamut3D_VR.html

URL 4.1 http://whatis.techtarget.com/
URL 4.2 http://scv.bu.edu/SCV/Tutorials/ImageFiles/
image101.html
URL 4.3 http://www.britannica.com/search?query=receptor&ct
URL 4.4 http://www.pcnineoneone.com/howto/hex1.html
URL 4.5 http://www.howstuffworks.com/scanner.htm
URL 4.6 http://www.kodak.com/US/en/digital/dlc/book3/chapter2/
index.shtml
URL 4.7 http://homepages.borland.com/efg2lab/Graphics/Colors/
ShowImage.htm

URL 5.1 http://www.pcworld.com/resource/printable/article/
0,aid,31050,00.asp
URL 5.2 http://www.internetnews.com/prod-news/article/
0,,9_809081,00.html
URL 5.3 http://www.pctechguide.com/06crtmon.htm
URL 5.4 http://www.pctechguide.com/07panels.htm
URL 5.5 http://www.sharp.co.jp/sc/library/lcd_e/index_2e.htm
URL 5.6 http://www.pctechguide.com/07pan2.htm
URL 5.7 http://www.pixtech.com/tech/tech.htm
URL 5.8 http://www.howstuffworks.com/projection-tv5.htm
URL 5.9 http://www.ecnmag.com/ecnmag/issues/2000/
07012000/PRODUCT_TECHNOLOGY_HIGHLIGHT/
ec07pth900.asp
URL 5.10 http://www.eink.com/
URL 5.11 http://www.parc.xerox.com/dhl/projects/gyricon/
URL 5.12 http://www.adobe.com/products/postscript/main.html
URL 5.13 http://www.canon.com/technology/bj/index.html
URL 5.14 http://www.dotprint.com/technology/digital_printing/
URL 5.15 http://www.ldr.com/products_new/indigo.shtml
URL 5.16 http://www.adobe.com/products/acrobat/adobepdf.html
URL 5.17 http://www.color.org/
URL 5.18 http://www.w3.org/Graphics/SVG/Overview.htm8

URL 6.1 http://www.lynda.com/hexh.html
URL 6.2 http://www.visibone.com/colorlab/colortest.html

URL 7.1 http://www.caris.com/S-57/ecdis_display.html

Glossary of common graphic file formats

(main source URL 4.1)

PostScript and PostScript-related formats

PostScript

PostScript (PS) is a so-called PDL (Page Description Language), introduced into Desk Top Publishing (DTP) in 1985 by software developer Adobe. It is a higher programming language that enables the graphic output of complete documents on a raster output device, e.g. printer or display screen. PostScript describes the layout, font information, and graphics of printed and displayed pages using object-oriented information instead of pixel-oriented information. Object-oriented structures (arbitrary shapes) consist of lines, circles, squares, rectangles and complex curves. Other features that are included are:

- painting primitives that permit a shape to be outlined with lines of any thickness, filled with any colour, or used as a clipping path to crop any other graphics;
- full integration of text and graphics: text characters are treated as graphical shapes;
- sampled raster images (e.g. satellite imagery): PS provides a number of facilities to control the rendering of such images on an output device;
- a general coordinate system facility that supports all combinations of linear transformation including translation, scaling, rotation, reflection and skewing. These transformations apply uniformly to all elements of a page description including text, graphical shapes and sampled images.

Many word processing, paint, CAD and other systems support this type of page description. These include CorelDRAW,

---

Adobe Illustrator, Macromedia FreeHand, QuarkXPress, Adobe Pagemaker, Microsoft Word and GIS packages such as PC MicroStation, ArcView and Atlas GIS. When a program supports PS, the print command of the program activates a PS driver that translates the internal program codes into PS program codes. This program code is written in ASCII format, which enables exchange of documents between all kinds of platforms.

For printed output, a PS interpreter translates the PS codes into instructions for an attached PS printer. The instructions from the PS interpreter are converted into raster data by special software, a Raster Image Processor (RIP), built into the output device. The PS interpreter and the RIP together are treated as a 'black box' by the application, i.e. they perform their functions automatically. PostScript is hardware independent. This means that any output device can be used if it is equipped with a RIP. The RIP can also be in the form of a separate software package. The RIP automatically takes into account the highest possible resolution of the available output device.

EPS (.eps) (Encapsulated PostScript)

The file format for the PostScript language. EPS uses a combination of PostScript commands and raster formats. Data in an EPS file is encoded in a subset of the PostScript Page Description Language and then 'encapsulated' in the EPS standard format for portable interchange between applications and platforms. An EPS file is also a special PostScript file that may be included in a larger PostScript language document.

PDF (.pdf) (Portable Document Format)

The PDF format was developed by Adobe, Inc. with the specific purpose of cross-platform document exchange. PDF strongly leans on PostScript, or better stated, it is PostScript based. Once a document is in PDF format, any user using the free Acrobat Reader Software can view, print and search the document. PDF documents retain the original formatting, layout, fonts and graphics, regardless of what program the document was created in. You can even zoom in on PostScript artwork without any degradation in quality.

Raster file formats

Bitmap (.bmp) (Bit-Mapped Graphic)

A graphic image formed by a pattern of pixels and limited in resolution to the maximum resolution of the display or printer on which it is displayed. Bit-mapped graphics are produced by paint programs such as MacPaint, SuperPaint, GEM Paint, PC Paintbrush, and some scanning programs. The resulting graphics may have aliasing (the undesirable jagged or stair-stepped appearance of diagonal lines in computer-generated images) caused by the square pixels. Bit-mapped graphics files are large. Resizing the pixels to make smaller files may introduce undesirable changes in the image.

GIF (.gif) (Graphics Interchange Format)

A graphics file originally developed by CompuServe and widely used to compress, encode and exchange graphics files on the Internet. The LZW compression algorithm used in the GIF format is owned by Unisys. Companies that make products that exploit the algorithm (including the GIF format) need to license its use from Unisys. GIF is mostly used for graphics that include mainly flat colours and text, so it is ideal for maps.

JPEG (.jpg) (Joint Photographic Experts Group)

A graphics format that is ideal for complex pictures of natural, real-world scenes, including photographs, realistic artwork, and paintings, but not well suited to line drawings, text, or simple cartoons. The compression uses a known property of human vision, namely that small hue changes are less noticeable than changes in lightness. JPEG allows a trade-off between image quality and file size. There is a visible effect in the image only if very high compression ratios, that bring down the file size dramatically, are chosen. A JPEG compression is 'lossy', meaning that not all of the original data are recovered on decompression. The JPEG scheme includes 29 distinct coding processes although a JPEG implementor may not use them all.

PICT

A Macintosh graphics file format originally developed for the MacDraw program. It can be a purely bitmap graphic, but PICT

---

files consist also of separate graphics objects, such as lines, arcs, ovals or rectangles, each of which you can independently edit, size, move or colour.

PNG (.png) (Portable Network Graphics)

PNG is a file format for image compression that, in time, is expected to replace the Graphics Interchange Format (GIF) that is widely used on today's Internet. The PNG format was developed by an Internet committee expressly to be patent-free (the GIF format is owned by Unisys). It provides a number of improvements over the GIF format.

Like a GIF, a PNG file is compressed in lossless fashion (meaning all image information is restored when the file is decompressed during viewing). Typically, an image in a PNG file can be 10% to 30% more compressed than in a GIF format.

The PNG format includes these features:

- you can not only make one colour transparent, but also control the degree of transparency (this is also called 'opacity');
- interlacing of the image is supported and is faster in developing than in the GIF format;
- gamma correction allows you to 'tune' the image in terms of colour brightness required by specific display manufacturers;
- images can be saved using True Color as well as in the palette and grey-scale formats provided by the GIF.

TIFF (.tif) (Tagged Image File Format)

The TIFF format was developed in 1986 by an industry committee chaired by the Aldus Corporation (now part of Adobe Software). Microsoft and Hewlett-Packard were among the contributors to the format. One of the most common graphic image formats, TIFF files are commonly used in desktop publishing, faxing, 3-D applications, and medical imaging applications. TIFF can simulate grey-scale shading.

WMF (.wmf) (Windows Metafile Format)

A file format for exchanging graphics among Windows applications. WMF files can also hold vector data.

Vector file formats

DXF (.dxf) (Data Exchange File)
A format created by AutoDesk. Almost all PC-based CAD systems support DXF.

HPGL (.plt) (Hewlett-Packard Graphics Language)
One of the oldest file formats. Although not very sophisticated it is supported by many PC-based graphics products.

PICT
A Macintosh graphics file format for exchanging graphics among Macintosh applications. PICT files consist of separate graphics objects such as lines, arcs, ovals or rectangles, each of which you can independently edit, size, move or colour. They can also contain bitmap graphics.

SVG (Scalable Vector Graphics)
SVG is the mathematical description of an image as an application of the Extensible Markup Language (XML) in the Web environment. SVG allows for three types of graphic objects: vector graphic shapes (e.g., paths consisting of straight lines and curves), images and text. The SVG format allows the viewing of an image on a computer display of any size and resolution.

WMF (.wmf) (Windows Metafile Format)
A file format for exchanging graphics among Windows applications. WMF files can also hold bit-mapped images.

Index

J

Joint Photographic Experts Group (JPEG), 60–61, 101–102, 155
  Internet, 104

L

Laser printer, 90–91
  compared to other printing methods, 82, 114
  for GIS output, 1–2
  printed colour charts, 116–121
Light-Emitting Diode (LED), 73, 79
  scanners, 58
Lightness, 24–26
  CIELUV colour space, 47
  colour cube, 38
  colour selection, 134, 140–141
  colour spaces, 32, 134
  density, 115
  eye sensitivity, 127–128
  HLS colour space, 40–43
  HSV colour space, 40–43
  ITC colour chart, 118, 123, 125–126, 134
  scales, 27, 134–137, 146
  visual variable, 2, 5, 29, 132, 144
Liquid Crystal Display (LCD), 73–76
  compared to other displays, 68, 78–79
  as GIS interface, 66–67
Lookup table (LUT), 71
  colour management, 121
  palettes, 107
Lpi, 59
  screen tints, 93, 96
Luminance, 38
  CIE chromaticity diagram, 45
  CIELUV colour space, 46–47
  CRT display quality, 72
  HLS colour space, 39–43, 148

M

Moiré pattern, 94–95
  stochastic screen tints, 97, 111, 118
Monitors, 68–73
  additive colour mixing, 15, 41, 64

colour selection, 132
relation to other colour spaces, 37, 40, 41, 48